ROCK CLIMBING BASICS

ROCK CLIMBING BASICS

TURLOUGH JOHNSTON

WITH PHOTOGRAPHY BY
MADELEINE HALLDÉN

STACKPOLE
BOOKS

published by
STACKPOLE BOOKS
5067 Ritter Road
Mechanicsburg, PA 17055

Library of Congress Cataloging-in-Publication Data
Johnston, Turlough
    Rock climbing basics / Turlough Johnston : photography, Madeleine Halldén.
        p.   cm.
    Includes bibliographical references and index.
    ISBN 0-8117-2420-4
    1. Rock climbing.   I. Halldén, Madeleine.   II. Title.
    GV200.2.J64 1995
    796.5'223–dc20   94-38238
                                        CIP

Idea, design and production by Johnston & Streiffert Editions
Photography: Madeleine Halldén
Desk-top: Mikael Eriksson
Reproduced by Repro-MAN, Gothenburg, Sweden
Printed in Italy, 1995

Johnston & Streiffert Editions would like to thank the following climbers and gymnasts for taking part in the photographic sessions: Anders Ahlin, Karolin Andersson, Sander Anfinset, Cecilia Hultercrantz, Jenny Dahl, David Granlund, Tomas "Tummen" Gustavsson, Kristofer Håkansson, Lennart Kullander, Ulrika Nandra, and Lena Råberger. Furthermore, our thanks to the Olympic Fitness Centre, Gothenburg, for use of their premises.

Lena Råberger and Madeleine Halldén have been closely involved in writing the text, which has read and amended by Jan Lönegren and Kaj Sandell.

AN IMPORTANT NOTE TO READERS
This book contains much useful information about the sport of rock climbing. Before engaging in this potentially hazardous sport however, you must do more than read a book. The sport requires skill, concentration, physical strength and endurance, proper equipment, knowledge of fundamental principles and techniques, and unwavering commitment to your own safety and that of your companions. The publisher and author obviously cannot be responsible for your safety. Because rock climbing entails the risk of serious and even fatal injury, we emphasize that you should not begin climbing except under expert supervision. No book can substitute for professional training and experience under the guidance and supervision of a qualified teacher.

GENDER AND THE CLIMBER
The author is aware of the great number of women who are active climbers and during the preparation of this book has received technical advice and help from several. He hopes, therefore, that women readers will understand that his use of the masculine pronoun in the main text is merely a stylistic convenience and that the book is aimed at climbers of all sexes.

Contents

Preface

Rock climbing is one of the fastest expanding adventure sports today and it is easy to understand why. To face the challenge of what appears to be a sheer rock face, to find within yourself the physical and mental strength to overcome the various problems that arise and then to sit at the top and reflect on your achievement put you in tune with yourself and with nature. You have met the challenge and succeeded.

Climbing is a dangerous sport, but if you climb correctly, it is not as dangerous as many people think. The high standards of safety that have been developed over the years, with better equipment and a more thorough understanding of the forces involved, mean that climbing can be carried out with relative security. Concentration, routine and consideration for your partner's and your own safety are the kingpins of climbing safety.

Don't become a high achiever, constantly looking for a harder grade to climb or for a more spectacular move with which to impress your climbing friends. Go for a level that gives you maximum enjoyment and if you feel like trying something more challenging, do it for the sake of the challenge and not because you want to boast about it. Climbing is exciting, challenging, and rewarding, but above all it should be enjoyable. Never forget the fun aspect of this wonderful sport!

Glossary

As the book starts directly with two climbing techniques, we give a short glossary here to help the reader who is new to rock climbing. Words in italics refer to other entries in this glossary

Abseil (rappel): To lower yourself from the top of a climb with the climbing rope or another rope that has been brought along for the purpose. In America, the word "rappel" is used instead of the German "abseil".

Active: The active part of the rope is that part that runs from the *belayer* to the climber. It is also known as the live part.

Anchor: The security system anywhere on a route to which the *belayer* is anchored. Also, the security system through which an *abseil (rappel)* rope runs. The top anchor is the anchor at the top of a climb, the ground anchor (or ground stance) is that at the bottom.

Back line: The rope or tape *sling* that runs from the back to the *anchor* point. Must always be kept taut.

Belay: To secure your climbing partner by holding one end of the climbing rope, which first runs through an *anchor* or *running belay* and then is attached to his or her harness.

Belay brake: Also known as belay plate. A piece of equipment that is connected to the rope to supply friction to lock the rope and arrest a climber's fall.

Belayer: One who belays when *top-roping*. The belayer who belays during lead climbing is known as the *second*.

Bolt: A metal bolt drilled into the rock for use as an *anchor* or an anchor point for a *running belay*. The use of bolts is forbidden in many areas, and some climbers consider them unethical.

Brake hand: The hand that holds the rope on the side of the *belay brake* that is opposite to the climber. When the brake hand moves the *passive* part of the rope into a certain position, the belay brake locks the rope and arrests the climber's fall.

Calls: The verbal signals that climbers use to communicate with one another.

Carabiner: Also known as karabiner, biner or even krab. An alloy connection between a *wedge* and the climbing rope. May be *locking (screwgate)* or *snaplink*.

Cleaning tool: A metal tool used to extract *protection* that has become stuck in a crack in the rock.

Descender (descendeur): Also known as a figure-eight descender. Used to control the speed of an *abseil (rappel)* descent.

Fall line: The vertical line from the climber to the ground.

Leader: The one who climbs first and places *protection*.

Leverage: This is the name given to the action of the climbing rope on *protection* that has been placed. When the leader has clipped the rope into a *running belay* and climbed on, every time he moves, the rope moves too, and that action can work the protection loose.

Locking carabiner: A *carabiner* with a locking device that is screwed down to lock. Also known as a screwgate carabiner.

Multi-pitch climb: A route with several *pitches*.

Passive: The passive part of the rope is the part that is on the other side of the *belay brake* to the climber. The *belayer* holds the passive rope in his *brake hand*.

Pitch: The part of a route between two *stances*.

Protection: *Wedges* that are placed along the route to safeguard the climber.

Prusik knot: A friction knot that, when loaded, will lock on a rope. It is used when climbing a rope or when locking off the belay system.

Quickdraw: A short sling of woven tape (webbing) which is sewn so that there is a loop at either end into which a *snaplink carabiner* is clipped. Used for extending protection to avoid *rope drag* or *leverage*.

Rack: The *protection* and *slings* that a *leader* wears when leading a climb.

Rack up: To select the *rack* and put it in order on gear loops on the harness or on a *sling*.

Rappel: See *abseil*.

Rope drag: This is the friction caused by the rope rubbing against the rock face or on a *carabiner* in a *running belay*, if it runs through the carabiner at a sharp angle. Rope drag can make it very hard to handle the rope, especially when a lot of rope is out.

Running belay: Protection pieces placed along the climbing route, always extended by a *sling* or a *quickdraw*, into which the rope is clipped.

Screwgate carabiner: See *locking carabiner*.

Second: The one who belays the *leader* in a lead climb.

Single-pitch climb: A route consisting of one *pitch*. It is never longer than the length of the rope.

Sling: Loop of woven tape (webbing) or rope of varying lengths. Slings are used for many purposes in climbing, for instance as part of anchor systems or to extend *running belays*. Also known as a runner or an extender.

Snaplink carabiner: A carabiner with a spring-loaded gate that snaps shut. It cannot be locked and is therefore not as safe as a *locking (screwgate)* carabiner.

Stance: Where the belayer is attached to an anchor. A stance can be at the bottom of a route (where it is called the ground stance), at its top, or anywhere along a route where there is a suitable ledge or suchlike on which to establish the stance.

Top-roping: Climbing while belayed through an anchor at the top of the climb.

Wedge: The name given to wedge-shaped metal pieces that are placed as *protection*. Depending on their manufacture, design and size, they may be called chocks, rocks, nuts, tapers or any of several other names.

Chapter 1

Top-roping

A safe way for beginners to learn the basic techniques, as the climber is belayed from below through an anchor at the top of the climb.

Top-rope climbing, also known as slingshot-belay climbing, allows the climber to be belayed via a top anchor by a belayer on the ground. The top anchor functions like an overhead pulley. We cover top-roping first in the book because it is the perfect method for the beginner to get to know the basic techniques and equipment used in rock climbing. However, consider top roping as the first step in learning what real climbing is all about, namely leading a climb, which is the subject of the next chapter.

An anchor known as the top anchor is set up at the top of the climb. The rope runs from the belayer on the ground through the carabiner on the top anchor and back down to the climber (the rope then looks like a tensioned sling, hence the method's other name). Should the climber fall, the belayer can arrest and hold the fall by locking off the rope in his belay brake.

If the belayer is considerably lighter than the climber, he must tie himself securely to an anchor at ground level (a ground anchor) so that he is not pulled up by a fall. Otherwise the belayer's weight combined with the length of the rope and its friction through the top anchor is usually sufficient to combat the force exerted on him by a fall.

The top anchor

The first step is to establish the top anchor, and this is usually done by the one who is going to climb first, while the belayer is setting up the ground stance. The climber walks to the top of the pitch with the climbing rope and the gear needed for the top anchor. At the top, solid anchor points are chosen, for instance a sturdy, deep-rooted tree, a rock horn or a suitable crack in the rock. If you choose a tree, its trunk should be at least so thick that you cannot encircle it with your hands.

A TOP ANCHOR
(Above left) A wedge firmly seated in a crack provides a sound anchor point for the pink sling. The wedge must always work in the direction of pull.

(Above) Another wedge in a crack anchors the purple sling.

(Left) The turquoise sling runs further back to a tree trunk, where it connects to a shorter sling, girth–hitched round the trunk.

The top anchor must have at least three anchor points, in-dependent of each other. If there are no natural anchors available, the top anchor must be secured by protection pieces.

If a tree is chosen as one of the anchor points, a rope or tape sling is passed round the trunk and tied in a girth hitch and a carabiner is attached to the sling. Use climbing rope or tape for slings – never allow yourself to be tempted to use old stuff you found in your basement. The other anchor points should be chosen so that they all work in the same direction, i.e. against the direction of pull that would result from a fall. Should the anchor

(Above left) Overall view of the anchor with the tape/webbing slings leading back to the three anchor points that are shown opposite.

(Above right) The locking carabiner attached to all three slings, just before it is dropped over the edge. The climbing rope is clipped into the locking carabiner. An ordinary (snaplink) carabiner should always be used with the locking carabiner as an extra safety precaution.

(Centre right) The locking carabiner and the climbing rope now hang well over the edge, so that the carabiner cannot be damaged by the rock edge when pressure is put on the rope.

points not work in the same direction and one of them gives, then the falling climber would swing like a pendulum as soon as the fall is arrested. The pull on the remaining anchor points can then be so powerful that they can be dislodged.

The tape or rope slings that run from the anchor points must be so long that the locking and snaplink carabiners that connect them and through which the climbing rope runs, hang over the cliff edge. Make sure that the slings do not pass over sharp stones or edges. Some climbers protect slings by running them through plastic or rubber piping or through an old piece of rope mantle of a larger dimension. You can also use rolled-up sweaters or rope bags to protect your slings.

The slings that lead from the anchor points to the top-anchor carabiners are best tied with retraced figure-eight knots (see page 59) if they are rope slings and with water knots (see page 61) if they are tape. The loops are then hung on the top-anchor carabiner system, which must be a locking (screwgate) carabiner with an ordinary carabiner as a backup (its gate should be

**ANOTHER KIND OF
TOPE-ROPE ANCHOR**
*Like the one on the previous page,
this consists of three independent
anchor points.*

*(Above left) One anchor point is
this rock horn, round which the
purple sling has been run. Just
visible is the rock on wire that is a
backup, just in case the sling should
slip off the horn.*

*(Above: centre and right) The tur-
quoise and pink slings are attached
to wedges in cracks. Double snaplink carabiners are being used by
more and more climbers, as safety
is an all-important factor.*

(Above) The slings run over the edge of the cliff and hold a locking carabiner through which the climbing rope runs.

(Opposite below) Each of the three slings are tied to double carabiners, and two of slings then run on to the cliff edge to secure the two carabiners (one locking and one snaplink) that will hold the climbing rope.

opposite the locking). The climbing rope is clipped in at its mid-point to the carabiners and both ends of the rope are dropped down to the belayer on the ground, who is first warned that the rope is about to come flying with the call, "Rope!" (Because the rope hangs from its mid-point, the climb can never be longer than half the rope's length.)

The ground anchor

While the climber is setting up the top anchor, the belayer is at ground level setting up a ground anchor, if he or his partner consider it necessary. Usually, the belayer does not need to be anchored against an upward pull, as there is so much rope out that the forces are not powerful enough to pull the belayer off his feet. However, if the belayer is standing in a precarious position or is considerably lighter than the climber, or if the climber is using a static rope, then a ground anchor is called for. The principles behind setting up a ground anchor are covered in more detail on page 24.

The belayer has always some kind of a belay brake, for instance a Sticht plate, a tuber or an ATC brake like that on page 46. (Belay brakes are discussed in more detail on pages 81–82.)

The climbing rope runs from the belay brake on the belayer's harness up through the top-anchor carabiners and back down to the ground, where the climber ties on with a retraced figure-eight knot and prepares to climb.

SETTING UP A BELAY BRAKE
The Sticht friction belay brake (or belay plate) is one of the most commonly used brakes available today.

The Sticht will be attached to the sit harness via a locking carabiner (either screwgate or twist-lock).

The belayer takes a bight of the climbing rope and threads it through the hole in the Sticht.

Warm up!

Warming up before you start climbing is just as important as warming up before partaking in any active sport. Your muscles work almost constantly during a climb and have to work intensively for short bursts during demanding power moves. If you have not warmed up, you are risking muscle strain (or worse). Make warming up an automatic part of your pre-climbing routine. The hike in to the rock face is often a good way of warming up, but you may also need to warm up by following some of the exercises on pages 112–113.

Communication

Good communication between climber and belayer is a vital safety factor in all kinds of climbing. The same climbing calls (see page 24) are universally accepted in the English-speaking world, which

He opens the locking carabiner and clips it into the bight. Then he screws the carabiner closed and checks carefully that everything is in order.

With the rope held like this, the friction between the brake and the rope is so high that the rope is locked. When he holds his brake hand so that the passive part of the rope is parallel with the active, the rope can run freely up to the climber.

makes it easy if you have to change climbing partners. All use the same calls, so there should be no communication problems.

The climb

The climb starts when the belayer, who is responsible for the ground anchor, says, "Climb when ready!", to tell the climber that he can start when he is ready. The climber replies, "Climbing!", to tell the belayer that he is just about to make his first move.

As the climber works his way up the rock face, the belayer pulls in the rope with one hand and then pulls it through the belay brake with the other, not allowing slack to develop and never removing the brake hand from the rope. The rope should be kept taut all the time, but not so taut as to hinder the climber's freedom of movement. If too much slack is allowed to develop, the climber will, if he slips, fall that much further.

Top-roping

The climber takes his end of the rope and ties the first part of the figure-eight knot.

The end of the rope is threaded under the leg-loop tie and through the reinforced loop on the harness.

The end is now threaded into the figure-eight (see page 59 for a more detailed desciption of this knot).

The knot is dressed so that all the loops are lying neatly and symmetrically and then it is drawn tight.

Anyone new to climbing should begin with a partner who is more experienced, not only because it is safer but also because one can learn from the other's experience.

Before starting the climb, it is important to have a general picture of the route and how it should be climbed. If the climb is long or has a crux, you should try to pick out in advance suitable spots to rest.

Three-point contact with the rock is an important rule in climbing and should be followed whenever possible. It means that three limbs (both hands and one foot or one hand and both feet) are in contact with the rock at all times to aid balance. Close cooperation between eyes, brains, hands and feet is the basis of good climbing. You should always have eye contact with your next hand or foot hold before you start your move. Scrabbling blindly about for a hold is a waste of energy. Once started, each move should be short, decisive and smoothly executed. Long moves will tire you out quickly and beginners need to spare strength for the final section of the climb.

Inexperienced climbers have a tendency to grip too hard with their hands in the effort to improve their balance or to increase their feeling of security. Again, this strategy will tire the climber unnecessarily.

When climbing, try to keep your hands no higher than your shoulders, and remember that your balance is better when your hands are out from your sides a bit. The same applies to your feet: feet that are too close together are not good for your balance.

When the climber reaches the top, he is lowered to the ground by the belayer who for this purpose uses the climbing rope running through the top anchor as a pulley. When the climber reaches the ground, he belays his partner, who now gets the chance to climb the same route. If for some reason he cannot be lowered down, he ties on to the top anchor, unties the climbing rope from his harness (but does not take it out of the top-anchor carabiners), and shouts "Rope!" to the belayer to warn him that he is about to throw down his end of the rope. Then he drops it over the edge, unties himself from the top anchor, and makes his way down to the ground stance, where he belays his partner, who now takes over as climber.

The belayer's duties
• Never take your eye off the climber, even if something much more interesting should be happening close by. If he moves out of sight, for instance after passing an overhang, move back from the cliff foot so that you can still see him. And always keep your ears open for an alerting call.
• Your partner's life is literally in your hands. Your concentration must be total: have you checked that the belay brake is the right

Top-roping

(Below) The climber plans the route he is going to take.

(Above) He makes his first move, keeping an upright body position and three points of contact with the rock.

(Opposite) The climber keeps as close to the fall line as possible, so that if he does fall he won't swing like a pendulum.

(Left) The belayer's grip on the active rope is firm but his brake hand holds the rope below the belay brake with an iron grip. His full attention is on the climber, so that a fall can be arrested instantly.

size for the job? Are you holding the rope correctly? Are you standing in a safe place?

• Make your position more secure by placing one foot against a rock or against the cliff face. If you hold the active (from belay brake up) part of the rope with your right hand, place your left foot against the rock, and vice versa.

• When you speak with the climber, speak loudly and clearly. Shout if necessary!

Another top-rope method

If the belayer walks up to the top of a crag and anchors himself there, he can belay a climb that is twice as long as that just described, because the rope does not have to be doubled. The belayer must then stand or, preferably, sit at the edge and keep the climber in view the whole time while taking in the slack. Safety precautions are the same, however: at least three independent anchor points that work in the same direction as the

The belayer lowers the climber from the top of the pitch to the ground by slowly releasing the rope through the belay brake. If he does it too quickly he can lose control of the descent and also overheat the rope. The climber sits comfortably in his harness, holding his upper body upright with one hand on the rope and parrying the cliff with his feet.

expected fall. An anchor here is a must, otherwise a sudden jerk can pull the belayer over the edge. To avoid this, the anchor backline must be tight up against the belayer.

* * *

Top roping is an excellent way to practise the basic techniques of climbing. To start with, the beginner should take it easy and keep to short climbs, say 10 metres (30 feet), in order to build up his confidence. When he has got used to these heights and feels at home with the various hand and foot holds, he can advance to longer and more complex climbs.

Top roping should be seen as an introduction to lead climbing and not as an end in itself. Intersperse top roping with some easy lead climbing, either as leader or second. If you spend too much time with the full security of a top anchor, you may find lead climbing frightening, and that could end your development as a true climber.

Leading a climb

Chapter 2

Leading a climb

All advanced climbing is based on leading. To climb in safety you place running belays as you climb. This is what most rock climbers regard as real climbing.

As beginners start to get the hang of basic climbing techniques, they will want to improve by trying increasingly more difficult climbs. Soon they will find themselves standing at the foot of a route that cannot be top-roped: the only way up is to lead it. This is where climbing begins to be really interesting!

The single-pitch climb starts at the ground stance, where the belayer (called the second) stands, and ends on the top stance, where the climber (called the leader) anchors himself to belay the second. The beginner will normally start on a single-pitch climb as the second, while the more experienced climber will lead.

An experienced team will usually choose a climb consisting of several pitches (a multi-pitch climb) and the two climbers agree who will start leading and how many pitches each will lead.

The climb illustrated is a single-pitch climb. The leader ties on to one end of the climbing rope, while the second ties on to the other. As the leader climbs, he places protection, known as running belays, and clips the rope into them, while the second remains alert on the ground, belaying the leader via the rope and the running belays. When he reaches the top, the leader first arranges a secure anchor for himself, then belays the second, while he too climbs to the top, taking out the protection as he passes and hanging it on his rack.

Climbing calls
We have already mentioned the importance of clear communication between climbers in a team and that there are a number

of standard calls that are accepted everywhere in the English-speaking world.

Beginners may find saying such an obvious thing as "Climbing!" a trifle awkward at first, but they'll soon get used to it and then it will come naturally.

Climbing calls must be made loud and clear. If the wind, distance or other circumstances dictate that you have to shout, then yell. Never leave your partner in doubt about what your call is. There is nothing more annoying (and even dangerous) than having to shout "What?" in a climbing situation that demands all your concentration.

The box on the right gives all the usual climbing calls, with explanations. If you are going to climb in another country, English calls will sometimes do, but it is a good idea to get to know the important ones in the language of the country you're climbing in. A French-speaking climber is not calling to his friend Pierre when he yells, "Pierre!" – he means that there is a rock hurtling down . . .

The ground stance

Among the second's duties is that of arranging an anchor at the ground stance, if it is considered necessary. As in top roping, a anchor is needed if the leader is considerably heavier than the second or if the ground layout means that a heavy jerk will pull the second off balance or into the cliff face.

The second sets up an anchor that is connected to at least three independent anchor points, all working in the direction in which the pull will come, should the leader fall. For instance, a sling round a rock horn and slings that lead from protection placed in a suitable crack are connected so that the load will be evenly distributed and a backline (a length of rope or sling) is clipped in-to a locking carabiner on the back of the second's harness. This backline must be kept tight at all times, to stop the second being jerked off his feet or pulled into the rock face.

Among the second's other duties is to stack the climbing rope neatly so that it runs freely to the climbing leader. The rope end that the leader ties in to should lie on top of the stack, while that which the belayer will tie in to should lie at the bottom but clear of the pile. The leader ties in with a retraced figure-eight knot (see page 59).

When the second has checked that the rope is correctly threaded through the belay brake, that the rope is correctly tied on to the leader's harness and that he himself is correctly tied to the anchor (if one was considered necessary), then he tells the leader, "Climb when ready!". While he was doing all this the leader was racking up, changing into his climbing shoes, considering his first moves and preparing mentally for the climb. When ready, he checks the tie-on for the last time and then warns the second by saying, "Climbing".

Calls

"Climbing!"
"I am starting to climb." This is used either when starting to climb or when continuing a climb after a rest.

"On belay!" or "Safe!"
Used by the leader when he has tied in to an anchor on a stance. The belayer can now take the climbing rope out of his belay device.

"Climb when ready!"
The belayer has the rope in his belay brake and is prepared to belay his partner.

"Watch me!" or "Tension!"
I am having a bit of difficulty here and may fall off. Be prepared and keep that rope tight!

"Slack!"
Pay out more rope. Climber to belayer.

"X metres/feet!"
You have x metres (feet) of rope left. Belayer to climber.

"That's me!"
Tells the belayer that the rope is tight on the climber.

"Up rope!" or "Take in!"
The climber wants the belayer to take in the slack rope that develops.

"ROCK!"
Something is falling. Watch out!

"Rope!"
I am about to throw down the climbing rope. Watch out below!

PUTTING ON A SIT HARNESS

(Top left) Hold the harness by the waist belt. Make sure you don't have it back-to-front. Step into the leg loops.

(Top centre) Pull the leg loops as far up your thighs as is comfortable. This is something that you will learn from experience. Some harnesses have adjustable leg loops. Fasten the waist belt. This particular harness has a double buckle. The first is threaded through the second.

(Top right) Tighten the belt.

(Centre) The most important safety measure: the belt is doubled back through the buckle. This is an absolute must.

(Right) As this climber will be belaying, she attaches a locking carabiner to the reinforced loop in the waist belt.

Leading a climb

While the second is setting up the ground stance, the leader is sorting out her gear and hanging it on the gear loops on her harness. This is known as "racking up".

Arranging a rack is a matter of personal choice. The gear she will choose will depend on the difficulty of the climb and the type of rock that she will be climbing. If the climb is new, then she will need to have a number of extra wedges, friends, quickdraws and slings, so that most protection situations can be handled.

Racking up is covered in more detail on pages 82–83.

The leader now starts up the cliff face and when he has climbed so high that protection feels necessary, say 3 or 4 metres (10 or 12 feet), he places the first piece.

Placing protection in a tapering crack

If the nearest crack tapers, then the most suitable piece of protection is probably a wedge-shaped chock, known as a wedge or stopper. First the leader checks the quality of the crack to ensure that the rock is not crumbling or otherwise weak. (It will have to take a lot of strain if there is a fall, so always check rock quality thoroughly.) He must think, too, of how a fall from higher up will act on the first piece of protection and place it so that it will oppose this. One might expect that the direction of pull on the first piece of protection would be up, but in fact the forces

(Above left) Planning the climb. Leader and second discuss the best way to climb the route. One should always have a clear idea of how to handle the climb and where the cruxes are before starting.

(Above right) The leaders puts on her climbing shoes. This is always done as late as possible, to avoid wearing them out and getting them dirty (dirt reduces the friction between shoe sole and rock). Also, as climbing shoes are tight and uncomfortable, it is best to have them on only when climbing.

work in two directions, up and down, producing a pull direction that divides the angle made by these forces.

Insert the wedge into the wider part of the crack and pull it down until it is firmly seated. Don't pull it so hard that the second will have problems in getting it out when retrieving it, but make certain that it will hold. As much as possible of the wedge surface should be in contact with the rock, to ensure maximum hold. Add a quickdraw or a longer extender (see page 80) to hold the rope away from the rock, to reduce rope drag and the danger of leverage. Clip the climbing rope into the free carabiner on the quickdraw or extender sling.

Wedges usually have two aspects, wide and narrow. The narrow may often be too slim to hold in a crack, but if it is inserted narrow and then turned to wide, it may achieve enough purchase on the rock to be secure. Otherwise, choose a larger size.

Placing protection in a parallel-sided crack

Hexcentrics, also called hexes, are passive, six-sided camming devices that can be cammed into parallel-sided cracks as well as used

in tapered cracks as described above. They are more versatile than the wedge, as they have more aspects, but they take a bit of getting used to. Page 77 goes into more detail on placing.

Protection in parallel-sided or flared cracks

If you don't have a hex that fits in a parallel-sided crack or if you are faced with placing protection in a flared crack, you must use an SLCD (spring-loaded camming device), such as a Friend, a Quadcam or a Camalot. These are good for flares up to an angle of 30°. The first such device to come on the market was the Friend, from Wild Country, and it became so popular that, to-day, climbers call all such devices friends.

A certain amount of practice is necessary to place a friend

(Above left) The leader prepares to place the first piece of protection.

(Above right)) Taking the carabiner with the wedges from the rack, she tests one of them for size in the crack, pulling down firmly. If it does not fasten solidly, she picks another size.

(Centre right) Having placed the right size of wedge, she hangs the cara-biner with the rest of the wedges back on her rack, takes a quickdraw, opens the carabiner and clips it onto the eye on the wedge wire.

(Above left) The leader now picks up the climbing rope, which is hanging from her harness, and prepares to clip it in the quickdraw.

(Centre left) Pushing open the carabiner's gate with her fingers, she slips the rope into the carabiner. The first running belay is now set up.

(Above right) The leader climbs on and prepares to place the next protection.

properly (see also page 78), and this practice should take place in controlled conditions before you start climbing. Once you have got the knack, friends are easy to place and to extract.

The running belay

Whatever piece of protection you place, it must be attached to a wire, tape or rope loop with a snaplink carabiner. This can then be extended, as described above, by adding a quickdraw or an extender sling before clipping onto the climbing rope.

The climbing rope now runs freely from the leader's harness through the carabiner on the first piece of protection and down via the belay brake to the second's harness.

The first piece now in place, the leader continues the climb, placing new protection where necessary, but first let's look at some of the one-handed skills the climber needs to have.

One-handed skills

Much of a climber's work is done with one hand, while the other is used to improve balance by holding on to the rock – as part of the necessary three-point contact with the rock, already discussed. Placing protection, adding an extender and clipping in the rope with one hand may sound easy, but it requires practice.

Here are some of the movements the climber needs to be able to carry out with one hand, while steadying himself with the other:

- Unfasten protection from the rack.
- Place the protection and pull until it is firmly seated.
- Unfasten quickdraws, slings and carabiners from the rack.
- Lift up the climbing rope to the carabiner.
- Open the carabiner and hang the rope in it (has to be done in one movement).
- Retrieve the protection, quickdraws, etc. and hang them back on the rack (the second's work).

To do any of the above deftly and right- or left-handed, you must practise. The beginner should spend considerable time practising both left- and right-handed work at home, so that the movements will be automatic on the rock face.

Straight rope

With the rope clipped into the first running belay the leader continues climbing. On the way up the rock face, he will try to place the rest of the protection in as vertical a line as possible, to avoid rope drag and leverage, extending the protection with quickdraws or longer slings, as already discussed. Place protection early, often and at the cruxes.

Protection is placed at regular intervals. A rule of thumb is every 2 metres (6 feet), but that can, of course, vary, depending on the leader's experience, the quality of the rock and the difficulty of the climb. A piece of advice often given to beginners is to place protection any time you feel insecure or feel that you can soon be in a fall situation.

Remember that it is easier to place secure protection if you are standing steadily on good foot holds and if you can manage to place it between hip and head level.

BELAYING

The second must be on constant alert and focus his attention totally on what the leader is doing. Bit by bit, he pays the rope out, always ready to lock it off in his belay brake, should the leader

By following as straight a line as possible up the rock face and by using quickdraws and, where necessary, longer slings, the leader keeps the rope from rubbing against the rock face (rope drag) and from working at the protection so that it loosens (leverage).

The longer the amount of rope that is out, the more the rope drag. It is important to avoid rope drag as much as possible, as it can make handling the rope extremely difficult, if there is a lot of rope out.

get into difficulties or even fall. He pays the rope out sparingly, keeping it tight but not hard up against the leader. Excess slack must be avoided, because if the leader falls and the second locks off the rope, the fall will be twice the distance to the nearest protection plus the amount the rope stretches plus the slack.

Another reason the second keeps a close eye on what the leader is doing is to see how each piece of protection goes in, so that he knows how it should be extracted when it is his turn to climb. Sometimes, of course, the leader will move out of sight and place protection there, and the second will have to deal with that problem when he comes to it.

At the top of the pitch

When the leader reaches the top of the pitch (the first stance), he first sets up an anchor and ties on to it. On no account does he untie from the climbing rope, because if he then slips while

The leader's safety depends on the second handling the rope and belay brake properly. She keeps her attention on the leader all the time. Her instantaneous reaction in the case of a fall could mean the difference between life and death for her partner.

Her brake hand holds the rope tightly. If her grip is even slightly loose and a leader fall subjects the rope to shock loading, the rope will run through her hand and cause rope burn, making it practically impossible to tighten the hold on the rope again.

setting up the anchor he will have nothing to stop a headlong fall. Once tied on to the anchor, he belays the second, who climbs the pitch. The anchor must, as usual, have at least three independent anchor points which, should there be a fall (if the second falls while climbing or if the leader slips and falls from the stance), will work against the direction of pull. A good anchor point is a well-rooted tree or a rock horn round which he runs a sling joined by a locking carabiner. As a backline connecting harness to anchor point, he uses a short rope sling or a loop of the climbing rope. The backline ties on to the locking carabiner with a clove

The leader reaches the top of the pitch. The first thing she will do will be to set up an anchor and tie in to it. When she is securely tied in, she can yell down to the second that she is safe. The call is either "Safe!" or "On belay!".

hitch, as this is easily adjustable. The backline must be tight up against the belayer, so that a sudden jerk doesn't throw him off the edge of the stance.

As further anchor points he may choose to place wedges in suitable cracks and then clove-hitched rope slings to connect that to the harness. All the anchor points should have equal tension, so the clove hitches are adjusted accordingly. Always check rock quality and consider the direction of pull when placing protection pieces.

When the leader is satisfied with the anchor, he shouts, "Safe!" or "On belay!" to the second. Only now does the second release

Leading a climb

the rope from the belay brake and untie from the ground anchor (if they had decided one was necessary). He then shouts, "Off belay!" or "Belay off!" whereupon he now becomes the climber and the leader at the top of the pitch becomes the belayer.

From the top of the pitch, the leader hears "Off belay!" and begins to take in the rope. When all the rope has been taken in, the second calls, "That's me!" to indicate that the resistance the leader feels is in fact the rope coming tight against the second. The leader now feeds the rope through his belaying plate and calls "On belay!". The second checks once again that he is properly tied on to the rope and calls "Climbing!" before beginning to climb the pitch, belayed from the top anchor by the former leader.

When the second reaches the first piece of protection placed by the leader, he unclips the climbing rope from the carabiner. Then, gripping the wedge's sling he works the wedge free of the crack and clips it onto his rack. (If a short extender has been used, it is usual to leave it attached to the protection, to minimize the risk of dropping it.) Once the protection has been racked, the climb continues, until the second arrives at the top of the pitch with all the retrieved protection.

The leader has pulled up all the slack rope so that the rope is tight against the second. Sitting down while belaying from a top stance is safer than standing. She has taken her climbing shoes off to rest her feet, and the backlines of tape can be seen stretching from her waist belt to the anchor. Those backlines could be more tightly stretched, but there is a good safety margin in the distance she is from the edge.

The belayer now puts on her climbing shoes (if possible you avoid belaying in climbing shoes, because they are tight and uncomfortable and because you wear them out more quickly).

She ties on to the end of the climbing rope with a retraced figure-eight and stopper knot.

"Climbing!" A clear call from the second warns the leader, who is now belaying from the top, that she is about to start climbing.

The second now retrieves the first wedge placed by the leader. Note that she takes the wedge and the quickdraw together.

Quickdraw and wedge are clipped on to the gear loop. Note the cleaning tool hanging from waist-belt loop. This is used to get the wedge out if it gets stuck.

Climbing on, she makes for the next running belay. Good holds, correct posture and concentration are important when retrieving a difficult piece of protection.

If too much slack develops, the call is, "Take in!" or "Up rope!" and the leader pulls in the slack. If the opposite is the case and the rope is too tight, he calls, "Slack!", and the leader feeds out some rope. At the top of the pitch, the leader shows where to tie on to the anchor, and the second sorts out the gear and hangs it in proper order on the rack. If it is a single-pitch climb, they either climb or abseil (also called rappel) down to the start-ing point. If it is a multi-pitch climb, it is usual that the leader now takes over as second and belays the new leader, who "leads through" and continues up. The climbing rope will have been stacked properly by the leader while belaying the second up the first pitch.

ABSEILING, OR RAPPELING

Abseiling, or rappeling as it is known in many parts, means that the climber descends by lowering himself under control down the cliff and then retrieves the rope by pulling it down. It is the method chosen by most climbers when there is no downward trail or when it is impossible to climb down easily. Climbing down is never as easy as climbing up, as among other things it is more

Safe up, the second ties in to the same anchor that the leader had set up when she made it to the top. Like the leader, she takes off her shoes to rest her feet.

The climbers can now share the sense of mutual satisfaction and achievement that a well executed climb gives.

If this were a multi-pitch climb, the second would probably "lead through" while the leader would become the second on the next pitch.

difficult to see the next foot or hand hold. And even if there is a trail down, it may be so long or rugged that it is quicker and easier to abseil/rappel.

You may also need to abseil/rappel if you have to go to the assistance of someone who is injured or for some other reason is unable to continue the climb. Or you may want to abseil/rappel down to sight or clean a new route.

Abseiling/rappeling is the most dangerous manoeuvre in rock climbing and demands total concentration and careful attention to detail. The list of accidents – many of them fatal – that have occurred when using this technique is long, and many élite climbers have been involved. Too many of these accidents have happened because of a faulty anchor or a badly chosen route, but poor concentration due to tiredness after a whole day's climbing is also a common cause.

The anchor

Setting a bombproof anchor for abseiling/rappeling is vital because your entire weight is going to load it. If anything gives you have no backup in the form of a belayer.

While setting up the abseil/rappel anchor, remember to stay tied on to the anchor set up by the leader on first getting there. If you have moved to a new position to set up an abseil/rappel anchor, always set an anchor for yourself first. Untie from this anchor only when you have connected your descender to and have full control of the abseil/rappel rope.

At least two independent anchor points should be chosen for the abseil/rappel anchor. Choose them with the utmost care. Never run the rope itself round an anchor point (for instance, a tree trunk or a rock horn) as the friction produced when you pull down the rope will damage it. There is also a danger that the rope might jam if it is passed round a tree or rock. Instead run one sling round the trunk and other(s) round the other anchor point(s). Thread the rope through the slings or tie the slings so that they support one loop and thread the rope through this. There is no need to use a carabiner, even if the rope would probably run more freely through it when being retrieved, but you don't want to leave more gear than necessary on the mountain. You must be prepared to leave the anchor slings behind, however, because there is no way to get them down once you have descended. But just because they have to be left behind does not mean that you should use slings that are of poor quality because of age or fraying. Your life is worth more than a couple of slings.

If the route is popular, then you will probably find old slings at the anchor. Don't use them – they may have been damaged by too much sun or burnt when those who set up the anchor pulled their rope down. Bolts that have been inserted there for the purpose of

providing anchor points must be checked carefully before use. Pull firmly to see if a bolt is well seated. Is the bolt sturdy? Pitons should be struck with a hammer to check the hold.

It is a good idea to provide the abseil/rappel anchor with a backup, for instance a wired chock with a carabiner that clips onto the rope. This backup should not share the load, however, and if the main anchor holds for the first to descend, the last person down takes the backup with them. If possible, the anchor should hang over the ledge, as the rope can then be easily retrieved by pulling it down. This is often difficult to arrange, due to the nature of the stance, so the rope has to run over the edge, with the consequent risk of fraying.

The rope is threaded through the sling to its mid-point. Tie a big knot, such as a double figure-eight, into each end of the rope so that there is no chance of your sliding off the end. Always ensure that the ends reach the ground or the next stance before you start. Shake a few metres of the doubled rope over the edge and then let it fall all the way, ensuring that the rope does not tangle. Sometimes the rope must be thrown (in high winds or on complicated crags) and should be thrown coiled.

The figure-eight descender

Make a loop of the rope and thread it through the big ring on the descender and then round its shaft. The smaller ring is clipped on to a locking carabiner that is attached to the harness's belay loop. Draw the rope through the descender until the middle point of the rope is at the anchor.

(Above left) This anchor consists of a tape slung round a sturdily rooted young tree a bit in from the edge of the cliff. A spring-loaded camming device firmly seated in a crack in the adjacent rock offers a good back-up, which will be taken along by the last man down.

(Above right) The rope is threaded through the loop in the tape and is hung near its mid-point (the yellow mark on the rope in the photograph on the opposite page). The rest of the rope is thrown coiled over the edge. Whoever throws the rope first yells "Rope!" to warn anyone below that a rope is going to come flying down.

How the abseil/rappel anchor is secured depends very much on the availability of secure anchor points. Here, cracks in the cliff allow the tape to be run right round an outcrop. This is not a loose boulder! Loose boulders, no matter how heavy and well-anchored they look, should never be used.

Take care that clothes, hair and suchlike cannot stick in the descender and jam it, leaving you stuck part of the way down.

The abseil/rappel rope

You can use the climbing rope for abseiling/rappeling, or you can use a lighter rope (say 8 mm). However, it is very difficult to control the descent with such a small-diameter rope, so this is not recommended for the beginner. Whichever you use must reach all the way to the ground or the next stance. Otherwise, you are going to have to climb back up along the rope!

The abseil/rappel checklist

When you are ready to start, both you and your climbing partner should do the following safety check to double-check that the system is OK:

• Is your harness on correctly?
• Is the waist belt folded back through the buckle?
• Is the locking carabiner properly locked?
• Is the anchor system bombproof? Check separately each anchor point in the system.
• Are you perfectly satisfied that the system will hold?

Stepping off

The most difficult part now follows: the step over the edge, from the horizontal to the vertical. This is a tough move, physically and especially mentally. Keep the rope taut with your brake hand (the hand below the descender) and stand with your

Leading a climb

back to the edge. If the main anchor's loop (see above) hangs over the edge, you will have to hold the anchor sling until you have passed the edge and then go over to holding the rope in your guide or active hand.

Let the rope slip through your brake hand at the same time as you back out over the edge. Your grip on the active part of the rope should be firm but not hard (holding the rope too hard is a typical beginner's fault). Don't jump, even if it looks terrific, because this will put too much sudden pressure on the slings. Back over step by step, feet below your hips and well apart, with as much sole as possible on the cliff face to provide friction.

Your body position should be half-sitting, with your legs almost straight but well apart, so that you can look between them to find suitable placements for your feet. Your active hand still holds firmly but not tightly to the rope, while your brake hand controls the gliding of the rope through the descender.

Stopping halfway

If you have to stop for some reason (to help someone who is injured or to unjam the descender), wrap the rope below the brake hand round your thigh three times. Try to get it as high up as possible on your thigh. This locks the rope and you can work with both hands free.

Once down

When you get down to the next stance, anchor yourself before you disconnect your descender from the rope. Of course, if you have descended to the ground, you don't need to do this. Then pull the rope to ensure that it hasn't jammed. If it jams then whoever is still up there must free it and make sure that it will run freely.

Finally, the first man down calls, "Rope free" or "Off rappel", to inform the others that they can now follow. As each new climber arrives at the stance, they tie in to the anchor before disconnecting their descender.

When the last climber has reached the stance and tied in to the anchor, he unties the big knots at the ends of the rope, ties one end in to his harness or to the anchor, and pulls down the rope. If he fails to tie the rope in, there is a danger that, should he drop the rope, it will fall all the way, leaving the climbers on a stance without a rope. With the rope safely down, the climbers prepare to abseil/rappel the next pitch.

Remember when abseiling/rappeling
- Tie on to an anchor while setting up the abseil/rappel anchor.
- The anchor system must be bombproof.
- Place a friend or chock as a backup anchor. Last climber down takes it along.

(Top left) Backing slowly towards the edge, the climber holds the anchor sling in one hand while feeding the rope through his belay brake with the other.

(Top right) As he approaches the edge, the anchor sling glides out of his active hand and he begins holding the rope. He has already begun to adopt a slightly more sitting posture.

(Below left) With as much shoe sole as possible on the vertical rock he is now in the abseiling/rappeling position, half-sitting with his legs almost straight and apart.

(Below right) Hanging still in his harness, the climber has locked off the abseil brake completely. To come lower, he must move his brake hand up so that angle made by the rope is reduced.

- The rope must reach down to the next stance or to the ground.
- The rope ends must have double stopper knots.
- The rope should not run over sharp edges.
- Make sure that hair, beard, clothes and equipment cannot jam in the descender or whatever belay brake you use.
- Don't kick or pull stones loose as you abseil/rappel. Those below you are in danger.
- Make sure that the rope can be pulled down afterwards.

The Dülfersitz

This emergency abseiling/rappeling method is useful if you have dropped your descender and have no other way of getting down. All climbers should learn it. No special equipment is needed, but you should have several layers of clothing, and do it very slowly, as the friction from the rope can cause skin burns that are most painful.

FALLING

Even if it doesn't *feel* natural, falling is a natural part of climbing. Often you have some forewarning, but it can also come as a total

THE DÜLFERSITZ
The rope runs between the climber's legs (yes, it is uncomfortable!), under the right thigh, diagonally across the chest and over the left shoulder, then diagonally across the back to the right hip, where it is held in the right hand (the brake hand). Left-handed people do it the opposite way.

(Left) The locked position. The right hand pulls the rope into the horizontal position.

(Right) The open position. The right hand moves the rope into the vertical positon. To achieve a faintly more comfortable position, he twists his body slightly to the right. This also allows him to see better.

surprise. However, *if* the running belays are sound and correctly placed and *if* the belayer does a proper job, you have every chance of surviving without injury. But you can never be 100% safe. Practise fall routines so that when it happens you know what to do, both as a leader and as a second.

The fall factor

Climbing falls are measured on a scale from 0 to 2, fall factor 2 being the most severe. The fall factor is the relation between the distance before the fall is arrested by the rope and the length of rope that is out. An example will clarify: Say that there are 8 metres (26 feet) of rope out between the second and the leader, who is 2 metres (6 feet) above the last-placed running belay when the fall occurs. The fall is 4 metres (12 feet) before the leader is brought to stop by the rope (that is, 2 metres/6 feet below the last-placed running belay). The fall factor is calculated in the following way:

$$distance\ fallen \div length\ of\ rope\ out$$

i.e. metrically $4 \div 8 = 0.5$ or imperially $12 \div 26 \approx 0.5$. In other words, a relatively light fall. A fall factor of 1 means a fairly severe fall, while a fall factor of 2 means that one should retire the rope if, moreover, its age, usage and exposure to ultra-violet light also tell against it. All ropes are rated by the UIAA to hold five factor-2 falls, but the safety-conscious climber should seriously consider retiring a rope after just one factor-2 fall.

The belayer's fall routine

Apart from trying to stay upright by hanging on to the rope and avoiding smashing into the cliff face by parrying it with one's feet, there is not much else that the climber who falls can do about the situation. It is the belayer who has the most to do.

If the leader realizes that he is getting into trouble he warns the second by yelling, "Watch me!" If he can, the leader should first let go with his feet, then with his hands. If he does the opposite, he may tip head over heels and fall headlong. However, there may not be time for a warning, which is why the second's constant and total attention is vital.

As soon as the second sees the leader fall, he whips his brake hand down and back, thus creating enough friction between the rope and the belay brake to arrest and hold the fall. His brake hand, therefore, must not be hindered by a rock or the branch of a tree. If the climber is being belayed from above, the belayer's hand moves up and back to lock the rope.

If the second has not had a firm grip on the rope with his brake hand, the rope will glide through his hand and can cause rope burn, causing him to let go of the rope altogether, with possible

Leading a climb

(Left) The leader feels that he is about to fall and yells a warning "Watch me!" to the second. The nearest protection is in the big, almost horizontal crack below his feet.

fatal consequences for his climbing partner. The importance of a firm grip cannot be exaggerated.

When the second arrests and stops the fall, both make a quick assessment of the situation. Is the leader hurt? What was the fall factor? Is the rope damaged? Are the knots OK? What has happened to the protection?

If the protection that was placed just before the fall was not solid or if the forces are so great that it is pulled out of the crack, the next protection in line will be subjected to strain from an even longer length of rope, and the result can be the so-called zipper effect, in which the protection is ripped out piece by piece.

If the leader is uninjured and there are no problems with his equipment, he can either climb back to where he fell from and continue to lead the pitch or he can be lowered off to the stance and start from the beginning.

An injured leader

If for some reason the leader cannot be lowered off and it is necessary for the second to get help or to climb up (or down) to

(Right) He falls, letting go with his feet first to avoid tipping over.

(Below left) The second has already whipped his brake hand down and back slightly in order to hold the fall.

(Below right) The fall is arrested and the leader parries the rock face with his feet, holding himself upright with his left hand on the rope. When they have checked the situation, he can either continue climbing or be lowered off.

assist him, the second must be able to release himself from the belay system without putting the system out of function, i.e. the rope must hold the injured leader in position.

Escaping the system

We show two methods and describe a third for the second to escape from the belay system while ensuring that the leader is still secured by the belay.

It is very seldom (hopefully never!) that the second needs to escape from the belay system, but when the occasion arises it is always an emergency. So learn how to do it properly, and practise it regularly, so that when your partner gets into trouble you can rise to the occasion.

TYING OFF
(Below left) The second locks off his ATC belay brake. Then he pulls a bight of rope through the carabiner. . .

(Centre right) . . . up past the belay brake and round the rope in a double overhand knot . . .

(Below right) . . . which he repeats at least once before pulling tight. This means that he has both hands free to escape from the belay system, if he needs to go the leader's assistance.

Escaping the system (1)

You are belaying from a stance somewhere on a multi-pitch climb, the climber has fallen, and you have locked off the belay brake as described on the opposite page.

(Top left) The belayer quickly ties a French Prusik to the live rope. He then ties a Prusik sling to the stance anchor and hooks that sling into the French Prusik's carabiner.

(Top centre) He then unties the knots locking off the belay brake and lets the Prusiks slowly take the weight of the fallen climber.

(Top right) He can now unclip the rope from his belay brake and descend on a second rope to help his partner.

(Right) The Prusiks take the full load of the fallen climber, with the second now free of the system.

(Left) Clip a carabiner in to the bight formed when you tied off the belay brake with a double overhand knot.

Escaping the system (2)

You are belaying from a ground stance, the leader has fallen, and you have locked off the belay plate as described on page 46. Happily, you had the foresight to set up a solid ground anchor. Follow the instructions that are illustrated on this and the opposite page.

Escaping the system (3)

A third method, not shown, is the following. If you have tied a double overhand knot in the rope above the belay brake, both your hands are free. Take a rope sling and tie it with a Prusik knot to the live rope. Connect the sling to the anchor with a carabiner and let the sling *slowly* take up the leader's weight. You can now unclip from the anchor and go for help.

Clip the same carabiner into the anchor line.

Unclip the ground anchor from your harness waist belt.

Now you can unclip the carabiner that attaches the belay plate to your harness, and you are free from the system.

The belay system now holds the fallen climber.

Equipment

Chapter 3

Equipment

Only the best equipment is good enough when it comes to climbing, but it must be used correctly. Concentrate on the essentials when building up a rack of gear.

Climbing equipment must be of the best quality to ensure that it will hold for all the wear and tear and sudden impacts to which it will be subjected. That is one of the reasons equipment is expensive. Safety costs, and you must be prepared to pay for it. Always buy new gear (never second-hand) and always make certain that it is made by a reputable manufacturer. Ropes, harnesses (in Europe), helmets, and a few other pieces of gear are rated by the UIAA (Union Internationale des Associations d'Alpinisme), and where this applies, always buy UIAA-approved gear. This organization runs a rigorous series of tests on gear and only when it has passed the test is it allowed to carry the seal of approval.

But even though you buy the most expensive, state-of-the-art equipment on the market, you must never trust it blindly. The responsibility for using the equipment correctly and for ensuring that it is kept in top condition is yours and yours alone. When the crunch comes, it doesn't matter how much you paid for your climbing rope if the knot you use to tie in to your harness is wrongly tied or if the rope has been allowed to get too old.

Equipment

ROPE

All climbers fall at some time or other, and beginners fall more often than experienced climbers. The beginner will, during the first year or two of his climbing career, fall many times as he attempts increasingly more difficult climbs, and this will certainly test the climbing rope. But even experienced climbers fall, and the respect they show their ropes is evidence of how important they consider them.

Construction and function

All climbing rope is of kernmantle construction. It is made of a core of plaited polyamide filaments in a sheath of woven polyamide fibres. The main load-bearing element is the core, while the sheath protects the core from abrasion, other damage and dirt. The core consists of about fifty thousand filaments of polyamide while the sheath is woven of about thirty thousand. Naturally, such a construction produces extremely strong ropes.

The rope's function is to arrest and absorb the force engendered by a fall. It must not only hold the fall, but also arrest the falling climber gently, so that the impact of the fall does not cause internal injury. Its elasticity, which derives mainly from the combined elasticity of the core filaments and the way they are plaited together, is therefore very important. If the rope had no elasticity a fall would be arrested so abruptly that the fallen climber would be injured and/or the protection would be ripped out.

Your rope is one of the kingpins in your safety system and should be chosen and looked after carefully. We have never heard of a rope that has been well looked after and is not too old breaking during a fall. In order for that to happen, the rope must have been damaged in some way, for instance on a sharp edge.

Choosing a rope

Rope is available in different thicknesses and in any length (as it is built in continuous construction and has no joints). The most normal diameters are 11, 10.5 and 10 mm for single-rope climbing and 9 mm for the double-rope technique. But whatever kind of rope you buy, check it for the UIAA seal of approval.

As a beginner it is difficult to know what kind or brand of rope to buy. Ask advice of some experienced climbers who climb in the areas where you will be climbing yourself or of the staff in your local climbing shop. They can certainly recommend brands that suit the local rock. Later, when you have climbed one rope into retirement, you will be in a position to make your own choice.

The perfect rope does not exist, as it would combine qualities that conflict with each other. For instance, a rope must be able

All approved climbing ropes have the UIAA stamp on them. This is a guarantee that they were manufactured to have a certain maximum breaking strength, stretch and absorption of energy. The stamp also states if the rope is a single or double rope.

This selection of climbing ropes from Edelrid illustrates the variety of colours and patterns that are available to today's climber. The four on the left are marked with a $1/_2$, which means that they are for double-rope climbing, which is an advanced technique not covered in this book, while the five ropes on the right are marked 1, meaning that they are for single-rope climbing.

KERMANTLE CONSTRUCTION
Climbing rope consists of a core, or kern, of plaited nylon filaments (a) round which a sheath, or mantle, of tiny nylon filaments (b) is woven. Each of the filaments runs the full length of the rope, so there are no weakening joins in the construction. The main load-bearing element is the core while the sheath protects the core from abrasion, dirt, etc.

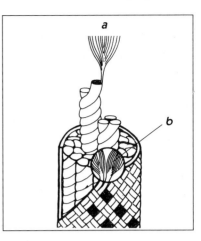

to withstand friction, which means that it should have a hard surface. But it should also have good handling characteristics, which means that it should be soft and pliable. A balance between these and other opposing elements means that the optimal rope is always a compromise.

Colours

Ropes are made in all the colours of the rainbow and usually have different patterns, too. The midpoint of the rope should always be marked either with a section of contrasting colour, by a change in pattern or with coloured tape. The midpoint mark is important because you must know where it is when you are arranging an abseil/rappel anchor. An abseil/rappel rope is always doubled: it is hung with its midpoint just to one side of the anchor sling's loop. Each time you retrieve it, you draw it down on alternate sides, thus ensuring even friction on both sides.

Having a particular colour or pattern on your rope is important when you are climbing with the double-rope technique and you need to call down to your second to give slack on one of the ropes. All you have to do is say which colour rope you want slack on. Then there is no risk of a mistake.

Another advantage of having a distinctively coloured rope is that you can easily pick out your own rope if it is packed with others, especially in poor light.

Waterproofing

When a rope is wet, its strength is reduced by 30%, the mantle becomes waterlogged, and some water will inevitably be pressed into the core by the bending of the rope. In the long run, the action of the water will lead to core damage. Some brands have impregnated mantles and even cores, which makes them specially suitable for climbing in a wet climate. Drying times will naturally be shorter for impregnated ropes.

Equipment

Coiling the rope

Handling a 45 metre (150 feet) long rope that weighs 3 to 4 kg (6 to 9 lbs.) requires practice. If you come to the rock face with your rope a tangled mess you are going to lose time untangling it. It's more fun to spend that time climbing. Besides, your partner is going to have to wait for you and will no doubt tell you what he thinks of that. Not a good atmosphere in which to start climbing. And should there be other climbers around to see, you'll certainly hear a few comments. Practise rope work at home until it comes easily, and you will save time, stress and embarrassment.

To avoid getting your rope in a tangle it must be coiled properly. The two most usual ways to coil a rope are the mountaineer's coil and the alpine, or butterfly, coil. Both methods are illustrated here.

Stacking the rope

When you get to the foot of a cliff and start organizing your gear, you must uncoil the rope and stack it neatly so that both ends are free, one for the leader and one for the second. Normally, it is the second's job to stack the rope, while the leader is preparing for the climb.

Place one end of the rope on the ground, a couple of metres away from your feet. Now stack the rest of the rope at your feet in tidy coils, the one on top of the other. When you are finished, you will have a neat stack of coiled rope, the bottom end lying clear of the stack and the top end ready for the leader to tie on to his harness.

Neatly stacked rope is a safety measure that ensures that the leader can climb freely and will not have to wait, perhaps in the middle of a difficult move, while the second tries to untangle the rope.

If the route is a multi-pitch climb, and the second leads through (which is normal procedure), it is important that the rope is neatly stacked at each stance. This is done by the leader, who has finished his pitch and is now belaying the second, who is climbing the same pitch and retrieving the protection. If the rope has been taken in and thrown in a tangled heap, it must be restacked before the second can lead through.

If the route is up a big wall with no ledges suitable for a stance, the leader sets up a hanging stance and drapes the rope in coils over his knees, so that it does not tangle. The second can then lead through easily and without unnecessary delay.

The mountaineer's coil can be carried over one shoulder or over the shoulder and neck.

Some people find it easier to make neat coils round their knees, especially if they are at a hanging stance.

Some climbers, especially those who are not so tall, prefer to coil the climbing rope round their necks.

When there are a couple of metres left, lift the coiled rope from your neck and make a bight of the end of the rope.

Wrap the rope end around the bight and the coil, as shown. Draw it tight. Repeat several times.

The end of the rope is taken in one hand, preparatory to threading it through the loop that is left uncovered (to the right of the climber's left hand in the photograph).

The end of the rope is threaded through the loop. Note that the other end is hanging freely.

The other end of the rope is now pulled tight, thus drawing the loop back under the wraps and locking the first rope end. The mountaineer's coil is now ready.

BUTTERFLY-STYLE ROPE COILING
1. Take an arm-to-arm length of the rope at its midpoint and drape it over the palm of your hand.

2. Take another length of the rope and do the same thing, making sure that the loops are of the same length.

3. Repeat until you have a neat pile of loops of equal length, hanging on each side of your hand. These are the butterfly's wings.

7. Thread the ends of the rope through the loop formed by the wraps at the top of the coil.

8. You can hold the whole coil up by the ends of the rope. Lift the coil up on to your back.

9. Separate the ends of the rope, one over each shoulder and cross them over your chest.

4. When you have a couple of metres or so left, start the process of tying the coil together by taking this in your left hand.

5. Wrap the last piece of the doubled rope round the coil.

6. Repeat this twice or three times, making the wraps lie snugly against each other.

10. Draw the ends of the rope behind you, over the coiled rope, to keep it in place.

11. Pull the ends of the rope back and tie them round your waist.

12. The butterfly coil is very practical as it is fastened securely to your back, leaving your hands free.

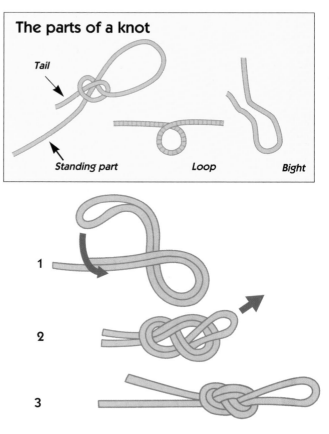

The parts of a knot

Tail

Standing part   *Loop*   *Bight*

1

2

3

Knots

It doesn't take long to learn how to tie the most common knots used in climbing but every beginner must learn this before actually starting climbing. The foot of the cliff is not the place to learn how to tie knots! Practise at home until you can tie them automatically.

Tests show that a knot reduces the breaking strength of a rope by between 20% and 40%. Despite this, a rope will hold for a heavy fall. Ropes only break if they are damaged, but a rope can fail you if the knot slips because it is badly tied.

Neat knot, safe knot

Before you set (tighten) a knot, you must always dress it, that is, arrange the knot neatly so that all the parts are parallel and do not overlap, cutting into each other. If you don't do this, you will reduce the breaking strength even more. Leave a longish tail free, so that you can tie a backup, for instance an overhand knot, tight up against the main knot as a stopper. This will prevent the main knot from becoming undone.

THE FIGURE-EIGHT KNOT
The figure-eight knot (photograph) is the best way to form a loop at the end of the climbing rope or anywhere along the rope when you want to tie in to an anchor.

1. Take a bight of the rope and make a loop of it.

2. Pass the end of the bight over the standing part of the rope and through the first loop.

3. Dress the knot and tighten it by pulling each rope in turn. Clip a carabiner into the final loop formed.

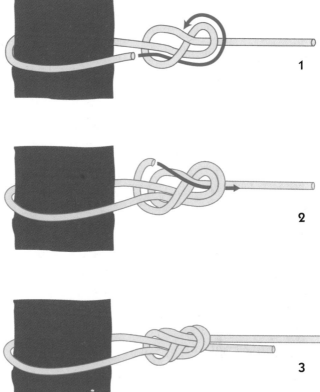

1

2

3

THE RETRACED FIGURE-EIGHT
The retraced figure-eight is used when you are tying the rope to your harness or round any object.

The first part of tying a retraced figure-eight knot means making a loose figure-eight in a single strand of the rope, leaving a long tail (see photograph).

1. The tail of the rope is passed round the object, for instance, a tree, and back into the knot.

2. Thread the tail through the knot, "retracing" its original path. Make sure to follow the original path exactly.

3. Dress the knot and pull it tightly. There should be a generous tail left over, which allows you to add a stopper knot such as the overhand knot, as a back-up, jammed up against the figure-eight. But if you have tied the retraced figure-eight correctly and left enough tail, there is usually no need for a stopper knot.

The figure-eight knot

This is the main climbing knot and it has many uses. There are two versions, the retraced figure-eight, which is tied to the end of a rope to form a loop for tying on to the harness or for tying the rope round an object, such as a tree trunk, and the normal figure-eight, for tying into the middle of the rope or for clipping into carabiners. The knot has a simple symmetrical appearance so you can easily check that it is correctly tied.

The retraced figure-eight is sometimes called the threaded figure-eight.

Equipment

The clove hitch

This is quick to tie and easy to adjust for tightness when connected to an anchor point (you don't have to unclip it from the carabiner to tighten up the rope to the anchor point.) Never use a snaplink carabiner with a clove hitch as the knot can slip over the gate and, if pressure is applied, force it open.

The clove hitch is always tied into the middle of the rope and the loops are dropped over an object before being tightened.

For absolute safety, you can back up a clove hitch with a figure-eight knot as a stopper.

THE CLOVE HITCH
1. Twist the rope to form two vertical loops, as shown.

2. Move the one loop over the other.

3. Drop the two loops over the anchor point (in this case a carabiner). Pull tight.

1

2

3

60

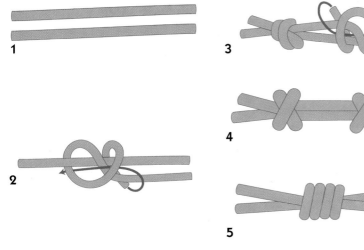

THE DOUBLE FISHERMAN'S BEND
This is the safest way to make a sling or to tie two ropes together.

1. Place the two ends parallel to each other, pointing in opposite directions. Let's call one end the standing part.

2. Wrap one end around the standing part twice to form two loops. (If you want to be extra safe, do it three times to form three loops.)

3. Thread the tail through the two loops. Pull the knot tight, leaving a long tail. Do the same thing with the other rope, making sure that the loops are made in the other direction.

4. Check that the crossed part of each knot is on the same side.

5. Pull each end so that the two knots are snug against each other, with no gap between.

The double fisherman's bend

Also known as the grapevine knot, this knot is used when you want to tie two ropes together, and for making slings from accessory cord.

It is especially recommended for tying together two ropes of different diameters.

The tape knot

Also known as the water knot, this knot is considered to be the only one suitable for tying together the ends of tape sling, even though it has been known to work loose. Long tails that are checked regularly for creeping are recommended. It is relatively complicated to tie and difficult to undo after loading.

Commercially made tape slings and loops are available and are neater and stronger.

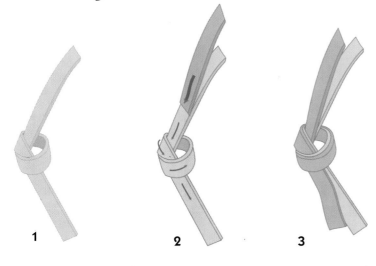

THE TAPE KNOT
The knot recommended for tying tape. Be sure to leave long tails and to check them regularly for "creeping".

1. Tie a loose overhand knot in one end, leaving a long tail.

2. Thread the other end through the overhand knot and trace it as shown.

3. The finished knot just before it is pulled tight.

Equipment

The Prusik knot

Called after its inventor Karl Prusik, this is a simple, effective jamming knot for ascending or descending the climbing rope or for temporarily securing it to anchors, for instance when tying off a fallen climber. With practice it can be tied with one hand. If the knot glides on the rope, retie it and add another coil of the loop round the rope to increase friction.

It can be difficult to undo, especially if the rope is wet. Also, the Prusik knot must not be shock-loaded, as it can then fail.

5

THE PRUSIK KNOT
How to tie a cord sling to the rope.

1. Hold the sling so that the double fisherman's bend is out of the way but not at the end of the loop, where it could interfere with a carabiner clipped into the loop.

2. Take a loop of the sling and pass it round the rope and push the other end of the sling through the loop.

3. Repeat this procedure.

4. Set the knot and tighten by pulling the sling away from the rope.

5. Check that the knot holds when pressure is put on the sling. If not, add another wrap round the rope.

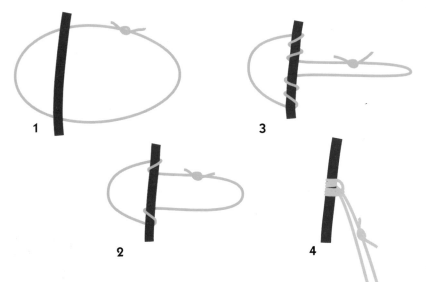

The French Prusik

The ordinary Prusik knot cannot be released under load, whereas the French Prusik can. It functions better than the ordinary Prusik when the rope is wet or dirty.

THE FRENCH PRUSIK
When making a sling for a French Prusik, make sure that it is not too long. Otherwise you have to wrap it round the rope too many times and the knot may twist when loaded.

1. Wrap the sling round the rope in spirals.

2. When all that is left of the sling are two small loops big enough for the carabiner, clip the carabiner through the two loops.

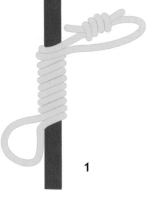

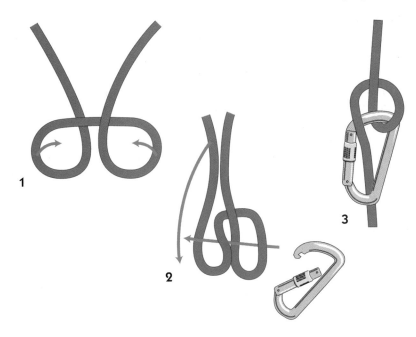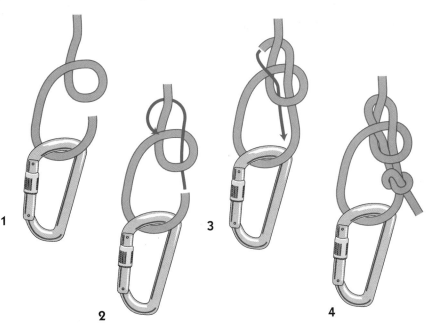

THE ITALIAN HITCH
Always used with a large carabiner, preferably pear-shaped, this is a friction knot.

1. Form two loops that touch the horizontal crosspiece.

2. Twist both loops in the same direction.

3. Clip a carabiner through the loops. Pull the tail of the rope towards you (the active part of the rope goes to the climber).

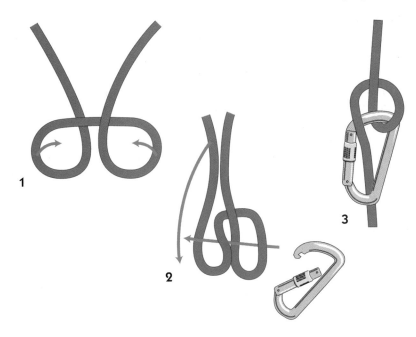

The Italian hitch knot, or Munter hitch

This is a friction knot which, when used with a pear-shaped carabiner (HMS carabiner), is good for dynamic belaying or for abseiling/rappeling (instead of a descender).

However, its very good braking powers are produced by pressure and rope-on-rope friction, which means that high temperatures are produced The heat can be so great that the mantle and even the core can melt. Also, if used carelessly it can produce kinks in the rope.

THE BOWLINE
The bowline on a coil can also be used for tying onto the rope.

1. Thread the end of the rope through the anchor. Form a loop in the standing part of the rope.

2. Thread the end through the loop from underneath.

3. Wrap the end round the standing part of the rope and back through the loop from above.

4. Pull tight and finish with an overhand knot as a stopper.

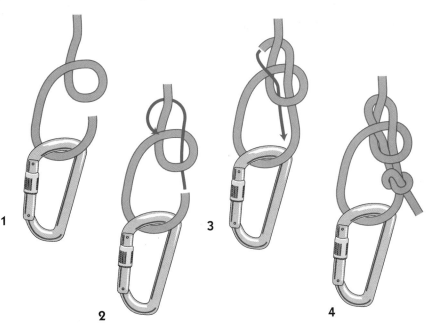

Equipment

Rope care

• Never stand on a climbing rope and never let it lie around where someone else can tramp on it. Embedded sand and grit will work their way through the mantle and when the rope is bent, cut into the core material.

• Never let wet ropes lie in a bag. Dry them as soon as possible in a shady, well-ventilated place. Hang the rope in large loose coils on a line, but not in the direct sunlight.

• Store the rope away from all kinds of chemicals, for instance from battery acid.

• Avoid storage in places with extremes of temperature, for instance in a parked car or in an attic.

• Don't let the rope lie in direct sunlight. Ultraviolet radiation is damaging.

• Store the rope away from sharp edges and do not compress it by storing things on top of it.

• Don't drag the rope through dirt or sand.

• Before and after use, feed the rope through your fingers a few times to check for damage. Slight irregularities reveal problems.

• Out of season, store the rope in large, loose coils in a dark, airy cupboard with an even temperature.

• Now and then, let the full length of the rope hang freely with a light weight at the end to untwist any kinks. Do this from a high cliff during a break in climbing, or hang the rope section by section from a lower height.

• The proper use of extenders will reduce rope drag, which in the long run causes wear and tear.

• After a fall, the load-bearing end should be untied and left to hang free for about ten minutes, to give the rope time to recover its stretch.

Washing the rope

If the rope gets dirty, especially with sand or grit, rinse it thoroughly in lukewarm water. Hang it in loose coils, away from the sunlight and direct heat, until it dries (it should take two or three days). If that does not help, wash again, using a mild detergent in lukewarm water. Rinse thoroughly two or three times. To dry, hang it in loose coils out of direct sunlight. Drying takes two to three days.

Some rope manufacturers claim that their ropes can be washed in washing machines and even tumble-dried, but as we have no personal experience of this we can only recommend washing by hand.

A most uncared-for rope . . . This has been trodden on by careless climbers, grit has probably worked through the mantle into the core, and every time the rope was bent, the grit was pressed further into the core. Or it has been cut by scraping to and fro over a sharp rock.

DATE	Meter climbed x 0.33	Abseiled/rappeled x 1.66 = Total	Total	TOTAL usage m
21 May	540 x 0.33 = 178	5 x 50 x 1.66 = 415	593	593
23 May	440 x 0.33 = 145	2 x 40 x 1.66 = 133	278	871
30 May	350 x 0.33 = 116		116	987
14 June	510 x 0.33 = 168	3 x 60 x 1.66 = 299	467	1454
15 June	175 x 0.33 = 58	2 x 40 x 1.66 = 133	191	1645
23 June	225 x 0.33 = 74	2 x 40 x 1.66 = 133	207	1852
24 June	440 x 0.33 = 145	4 x 50 x 1.66 = 332		

Rope retirement

How long active service should a climbing rope see before it is retired? The most obvious reasons for an early retirement are damage, such as cuts or severe abrasion, a severe fall (factor 2) or the number of less severe falls that the rope is rated for. *Always* retire a rope in these cases.

If a rope is not damaged, then it should be retired for age reasons. There are many interrelated factors that age a rope: frequency of use, type of rock mainly climbed, climbing technique, rope management, types of belay brake used, type of abseil/rappel brake used, rope construction, and climatic influences. Each manufacturer has recommendations: follow them.

Many climbers keep a rope log to keep a check on how many metres have been climbed, what falls have been taken, how many metres abseiled/rappeled, and so on. Edelrid has worked out a type of rope diary, which we show here. To evaluate the noticeable difference in wear and tear on a rope when climbing and abseiling/rappeling, they multiply metres climbed by a factor of 0.33 and metres abseiled/rappeled by a factor of 1.66.

Otherwise, the rule of thumb is that you retire an undamaged rope used for regular weekend climbing after two years. If it has been used infrequently (once or twice a year) and carefully stored, it should last up to four years, but if it has been used more or less daily during a season, six months to one year is enough.

Equipment

HARNESSES

The climbing harness is made of strong nylon webbing of different widths. Parts of the harness are padded for comfort. Check the webbing material regularly: if it becomes frayed, you need to get a new harness.

Your harness is your fixed point of contact with the rope. In the event of a fall, the harness and the knot that ties it on to the rope can be subjected to extreme loads, but the harness distributes these loads over the major muscle groups of the buttocks and thighs.

There are many different brands on the market but only three basic types. As always it is difficult for the beginner to choose a brand best suited to him and the type of climbing he will do. And again, the beginner should ask around, or get an experienced climber to go with him to the climbing shop to give advice. Most good shops have some arrangement whereby you can sit in a harness and test it for function, comfort and fit. Try several different brands before you decide. It should be easy to put on and take off, be comfortable, and have plenty of loops for your gear.

Some harnesses are two-piece, with separate waist belt and leg loops, so you can choose the parts separately to suit your physique.

The three types of harness available are the chest harness, the sit harness and the combination harness. The chest harness is not recommended for climbing, unless it is combined with a sit harness, as a fall concentrates all the forces in the chest area and if a fallen climber hangs for too long, he can suffocate. It is important the the fallen climber should not tip back or sideways, especially if he becomes unconscious.

One of Edelrid's all-round sit harnesses with double titanium buckles, two flexible, rectangular gear loops on each side, tear-out resistant up to 50 kg (110 lb), and adjustable straps to regulate the height of the leg loops.

The sit harness

The sit harness is the most common type, as it is comfortable, fashionable, easy to put on and take off, and gives the climber plenty of freedom of movement. With it on, you can even put on or take off a sweatshirt while halfway up a pitch.

Many sit harnesses have adjustable leg loops, which is preferable, especially if you are going to climb sometimes bare-legged and sometimes with several layers of clothing.

You hang your rack in the harness loops or on an accessory cord that you tie between a couple of loops. Some people prefer to have the rack on a bandolier which is hung around the neck and under an arm. We prefer to rack up on the harness loops, so that it does not get in the way when climbing.

One disadvantage with the sit harness is that if you fall and become unconscious you can be left hanging in a tipped back position. Should you be wearing a backpack you can end up almost upside down, and this can lead to internal injury and/or suffocation if you are left hanging there too long.

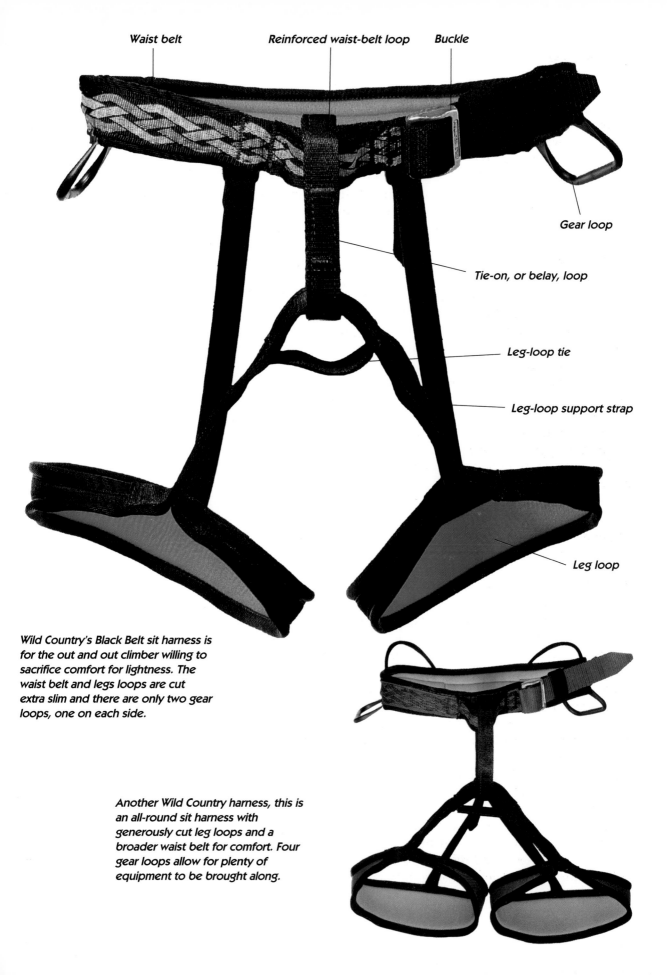

Waist belt

Reinforced waist-belt loop

Buckle

Gear loop

Tie-on, or belay, loop

Leg-loop tie

Leg-loop support strap

Leg loop

Wild Country's Black Belt sit harness is for the out and out climber willing to sacrifice comfort for lightness. The waist belt and legs loops are cut extra slim and there are only two gear loops, one on each side.

Another Wild Country harness, this is an all-round sit harness with generously cut leg loops and a broader waist belt for comfort. Four gear loops allow for plenty of equipment to be brought along.

Equipment

The combination harness

A harness that combines the chest and sit harness is without a doubt the safest harness for rock climbing, as it distributes the fall load over a greater area of the body (firstly over the large buttock and thigh muscles and then over the chest and back). If you fall heavily you will not jack-knife or finish in an upside-down position, even if you are unconscious, due to the fact that your tie-on point is higher up than on just a sit harness.

That said, it has to be admitted that almost all rock climbers use a sit harness, mainly for the sake of comfort and freedom of movement, but also because it has become the fashion. However, no sit harnesses have been approved by the UIAA, while combined harnesses have.

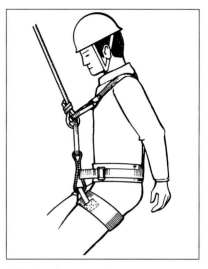

This drawing shows how the combination harness can hold a fallen, perhaps unconscious, climber upright after a fall.

Double back on the buckle!

No matter what type of harness you decide to go for, there is a vital safety precaution that must be taken when putting it on. The waist belt has a buckle that must be secured by doubling back the belt and running it through the buckle again, first over the near bar and then under the far bar. Leave a tail of about 10 cm (4 inches) at the end. Never forget to do this. An élite climber forgot this elementary precaution during a recent international indoor competition and fell badly, a reminder to all of us to check everything twice. Harnesses without buckles do not suffer from this problem, of course.

Tying on

There are different schools of thought concerning how the climbing rope should be tied on to the harness. Furthermore, different brands require you to tie on in slightly different ways, so you should always ensure that the manufacturer's instructions for tying on accompany a harness, when you buy it.

The leg loops of a sit harness are connected by a leg-loop tie which in turn is connected to the reinforced waist-belt loop or directly to the waist belt by a rising loop of webbing called the tie-on or belay loop. Some manufacturers, for instance Edelrid and Wild Country, have made this tie-on loop so strong that the rope may be tied directly to it. This is certainly true, and indeed their technical data is impressive, but climbers should still go for the more traditional method of tying on to the harness through at least two points.

This entails threading the rope end under the leg-loop tie and then under the waist belt before tying a retraced figure-eight in the rope.

Some safety-conscious climbers go for tying on through three points: the two mentioned above and then on the diagonal through the tie-on loop.

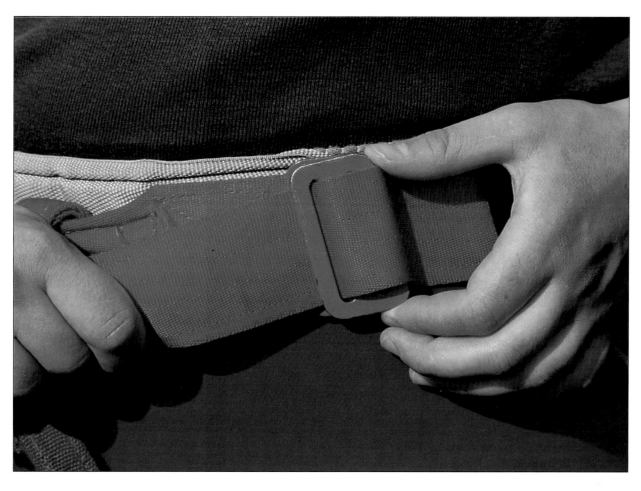

Doubling back the belt through the buckle is a safety precaution that no climber should overlook.

Should the harness have reinforced ears on the waist belt especially for tying on, the rope is threaded first through the leg-loop tie and then through each of the ears (important that it goes through both ears) before the knot is tied.

Finally, when the knot is tied, back it up with an overhand knot.

Tying on to an anchor

A locking carabiner clipped into the reinforced loop on the waist belt is a good tie-on point when you want to tie on to a anchor. If your anchor is behind you, you may prefer to clip the carabiner into the back of your waist belt (some harnesses have a second reinforced loop at the back, especially for this purpose). Tie the backline between the anchor's carabiner and your tie-on carabiner with a clove hitch or a retraced figure-eight knot.

Equipment

CLIMBING SHOES

Most beginners try their hand at climbing before they buy themselves climbing shoes. A pair of running shoes will do fine to begin with, but later, when you have decided to get serious about climbing, you will want to buy your own shoes. When you compare climbing with running shoes to climbing with climbing shoes you will be awed by the difference, especially at the amount of friction you can obtain on small holds with the latter. A foot hold that previously was extremely difficult with running shoes now becomes simple.

Shoe with a fairly high cut. The lace is tied round the ankle for extra support.

However, a good pair of walking boots for hiking to the rock-face, often over rough ground, is a necessary part of your climbing equipment. Climbing shoes are expensive and wear out quickly. Don't use them for hiking or walking about at the foot of the cliff. Don't even use them when belaying a leader. Wait until he has reached the top of the pitch, and then change to your climbing shoes.

Nowadays there is a wide choice of shoes for different types of climbing. There are shoes with pointed, stiffish toes for sticking straight into pockets, stiff-soled shoes for edging, low-cut shoes for higher steps, and high-cut shoes to support the ankle while jamming. Friction shoes have soles of thin, smooth, sticky rubber which is drawn a bit up over the edges in what is called the rand. This makes it easier to obtain friction in a foot jam or gain purchase in a corner.

Low-cut shoe with flex. Good for smearing.

When you buy your shoes, remember that they will stretch both across and along the foot. A good, tight fit, maybe one to one-and-a-half sizes smaller than your street footwear, is important to reduce foot roll on edges and to increase the feel for the rock. Shoes must feel like a second skin and when you stand in them, your toes should be pressed tightly up against the shoe. This will be painful until the shoes stretch and even then the shoes are never going to be completely comfortable. Many climbers take every opportunity to take their shoes off to rest their feet (for instance, while belaying the second from the top of a pitch).

Some climbers like to have socks, others wear their shoes without. It is a matter of preference (and climate) and doesn't much matter one way or the other.

Some shoes have metal rings in the upper eyes to enable them to be laced hard. This is fine, but be sure not to draw the laces so hard that a ridge is built between the eyes.

Lacing should form the shoe to the foot. This climber uses two laces to ensure a close fit. The shoe is kept clean by placing it on a walking shoe.

As mentioned, climbing shoes are expensive, so look after them well. Wash dirt and grit from the sole and rand after each day's climbing. Try to keep the soles clean during climbing, as dirt will reduce the friction obtained. If you climb on sea cliffs, rinse the shoes with fresh water after climbing, as salt can eat away at the seams and corrode the metal rings.

(Above) Medium-sized chalk bag with fibre-pile lining. The rims of the bag are stiffened by the webbing border round the top edge. A draw-cord is used to close the top when the bag is not in use.

(Right) The almost ritual act of dipping the fingers into the chalk bag before making a move. On the practical side, chalk dries and neutralizes hand sweat, which would otherwise cause a chemical reaction with the rock, making holds "polished" and thus more difficult to exploit.

CHALK

The chalk used by climbers today is actually magnesium carbonate powder. It dries sweat from fingers and palms and thus improves the grip. Some find that dipping the fingers in the chalk bag is a ritual that helps them gather their thoughts and charges them mentally for the move ahead.

Chalk is kept in a bag or pouch that hangs from the back of the waist belt. The bag should be fleece-lined to enable the fingers to brush off surplus chalk, and the opening should be kept open by a hard rim.

To chalk or not to chalk is a sensitive subject that is hotly debated in some climbing circles. Many deplore the unsightly white marks left by the chalk on the rock face, while some hardliners consider its use to be cheating. Chalk is a big help, so use it where it is permitted (always check this when you come to an area that is new to you).

HELMETS

This is another sensitive subject, even though there has been little debate. Attitudes to climbing helmets are the same as attitudes to cycle helmets: they *should* be worn, but they *are* ugly and uncomfortable. And then there are those who say that if you get hit by a big piece of rock, it doesn't matter if you are wearing a helmet or not, does it?

People who climb in areas where the rock is hard and clean usually do not bother about getting helmets. That's fine until the day someone drops just a micro-nut on your head from way above or you try climbing in an area of crumbling sandstone . . .

There is no point in having a helmet you don't wear. Nowadays helmets are light (many below a $\frac{1}{2}$ kg, 1 lb) yet have a high degree of safety and wearing them is becoming accepted practice among safety-conscious climbers.

(Above) A good helmet should be light but strong, with ventilation to let sweat escape. One drop of sweat causes 1.5 litres (3 pints) of vapour, so there is no doubt that ventilation is important! The chin strap should be adjustable and there should be an absorbing headband between the climber's head and the outer shell.

(Right) Climbing on clean, hard rock like this may seem to make a helmet superfluous, as there are no loose stones to break off or be kicked over the edge. But there are other things that can fall, such as a piece of gear from a climber on the pitch above.

At the end of the day, the choice is yours. But before you make that choice, talk to someone who has been hit on the head by a pebble falling no more than ten metres/yards. No great damage done, perhaps, but a whole day's climbing lost by a visit to the local emergency ward for medical attention. It is like the cycle helmet: if you've been in a road accident once, you will always wear your helmet in future.

A good climbing helmet should be approved by the UIAA, sit snugly on your head, and come down a bit over your forehead. Its main purpose is to protect your head from falling stones, but it can even protect the head during a fall.

A light-coloured helmet will not be so hot to wear in the direct sunlight, and if it has ventilation holes to keep it cool, so much the better.

Straight-gate, 93x50 mm, 33 grams.   **Bent-gate, 93x50 mm, 33 grams**

Snaplink carabiners in a quickdraw. Straight-gate carabiners usually go at the top end of a quickdraw while bent-gates are used for the bottom end.

The range of snaplink carabiners shown on this page would do for most normal rock climbing. They are shown in both silver and another colour.

Straight-gate, 99x53 mm, 46 grams   **Bent-gate 99x53 mm, 48 grams**

Straight-gate, 109x52 mm, 56 grams

CARABINERS

The carabiner (also spelled karabiner) is the link between the various parts of the climber's safety system: the rope, the anchor, the runner, and the belay brake. There are two types, snaplink (or ordinary) and locking (also known as screwgate).

Carabiners are forged from aluminium alloy and are usually oval-, D- or pear-shaped. D-shaped carabiners are considered strongest because the loading is applied along the longest side (opposite the gate).

In recent years there has been a move towards ever lighter, hollow carabiners, encouraged by big-wall climbers who want to have the lightest possible equipment. Such carabiners are not UIAA-approved and are too flimsy to be recommended. They are OK for hanging your chalk bag on, but not for much else.

Aluminium oxidises easily, especially in contact with water. Oxidation is first noticed when the carabiner leaves a black mark on your hand. Light oxidation is not dangerous but you should always wipe your carabiners dry when you get home from climbing.

The snaplink carabiner

The snaplink carabiner has a spring-loaded gate that snaps into the closed position and that must be pressed to open. It is

Straight-gate, 114x73 mm, 75 grams. Silver only.

usually used to link a running belay to the climbing rope, but it can be used as an anchor if it is backed up by another snaplink carabiner, with its gate opposed.

The snaplink carabiner's gate should always point away from the rock to avoid its being opened unintentionally by the rope pulling it against a point of rock.

Bent-gate carabiners are quicker to use and are particularly popular in quickdraws, especially when you are working with one hand. However, some climbers are sceptical about bent-gates, as

shock-loading or twisting of the rope or sling has been known to force the gate open. Always back up a locking carabiner with a snaplink, for safety's sake.

The locking carabiner

The gate in a locking carabiner is also spring-loaded, but it is then locked by a threaded metal sleeve or a spring-loaded collar that covers the latch. This type is used for connecting harnesses to belay brakes, abseil/rappel devices and anchors, anything that demands the extra security provided by the fact that the gate on such a carabiner cannot be forced open by a jutting rock.

Locking carabiners can sometimes jam because of dirt on the threads or because you screwed them into a locked position while they were under load.

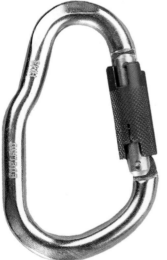

LOCKING CARABINERS
(Top) 99x53 mm, 52 grams
(Centre from left to right) 110x52,
67 grams; 114x73, 85 grams;
115x75 mm, 87 grams.
(Bottom) Twist-lock type.
116x75 mm, 84 grams.

Carabiner tips
• The gate is the weakest part of the carabiner, so you should avoid loading the carabiner in three directions, as a rope or webbing can slip round onto the gate and damage it.
• Retire any carabiners that fall from a height of anything over 4–5 metres (12–15 feet). Microscopic cracks can be caused by the

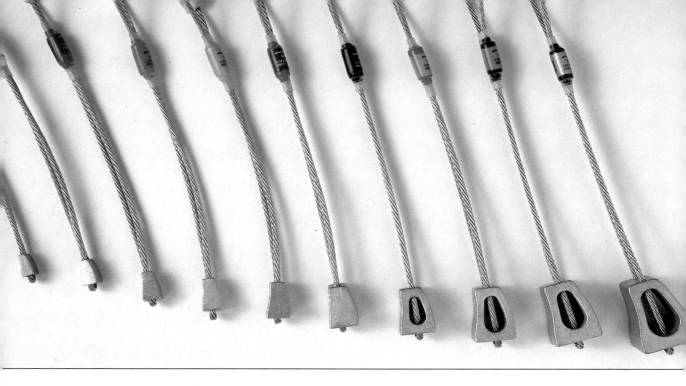

fall and you won't notice these until the carabiner is shock-loaded.
- If the gate is stiff or out of true, retire the carabiner. Never oil it. Dry graphite may be used, however.
- After climbing a sea cliff, rinse your carabiners in fresh water and dry them.
- Use slings that are long enough to keep the carabiner from being bent against a projecting rock edge.

PROTECTION

There are two basic kinds of protection, chocks and friends. They are inserted into cracks in the rock so that they fasten there. A short sling of wire, rope or webbing hangs on the protection and the climbing rope can be attached to this via a carabiner. Normally the chock sling is extended by another sling and carabiner to keep the rope away from the rock and running in as straight a line as possible from belayer to climber. This is known as a running belay, or runner.

In the event of a climber falling, the runners are subject to sudden loads and the protection must be able to bear this pressure. Placing protection well is therefore very important.

Chocks

Chocks, rocks, nuts, micro-nuts, wedges, stoppers, tapers. This kind of protection has many names but is basically the same thing (a forged piece of metal which can be wedge-shaped, straight-sided, with alternating concave and convex sides or with other variations on this theme). It is attached to a short sling which has at its free end an eye with a snaplink carabiner. Whatever the chock's shape the important thing is that, when it

Wild Country's rocks on wire range from sizes 1 to 10. Size 1 is 7 mm thick, 13 mm wide and weighs 16 grams. Size 10 is 30 mm thick, 31 mm wide and weighs 71 grams. Each size has its own colour code.

Wires on wedges are between 2 and 4 mm in diameter. They have to be both strong and flexible.

Rocks like these are universally used in cracks with a positive taper (narrowing in the direction of pull). As the pull can be outward as well as downward, the climber should look for a crack that prevents movement in either of these directions.

HEXES

Hexes can be used as simple wedges in tapering cracks or as camming devices in parallel-sided cracks and horizontal slots. In a horizontal slot, the hex should be placed so that the sling leaves the hex near the roof of the slot. When placed, the hex is cammed against the rock surfaces by a firm pull. A cammed hex is highly effective and the camming action resists rope drag.

(Above left) The largest size of hex is shown here being used as a simple wedge by placing it so that its transverse aspect jams in the crack.

(Above right) This hex has been cammed into a diagonal, parallel-sided crack.

is in place, the greatest possible friction is obtained, ensuring the best security available just at that point.

Chocks are available in different sizes, and often even in half-sizes, in aluminium, brass or alloy. The smaller sizes can be bought ready fitted with 1.5 to 4 mm wires and the bigger sizes with 5 to 8 mm accessory cord. Some brands only make wired chocks. These wires and cords are always fitted with an eye into which carabiners are clipped, as described above.

Hexcentrics

A hexcentric, or hex, is a passive, six-sided camming device with no side the same length (it is an "eccentric hexagon"). The advantage of a hex is that it offers several more aspects than a chock, so that you can place it in different sizes of cracks, including parallel-sided, horizontal slots. When placed transversely, it works in the non-camming mode, as an ordinary chock.

Hexes are usually fitted with accessory cord. When you buy hexes, check that the drilled holes are smooth. Burrs left by the drill will cut into the cord very easily.

Equipment

Spring-loaded camming devices

SLCDs have up to four spring-loaded cams that work independently of each other. When the retractor bar is pulled, the cams close, and when it is released, they open out, biting into the rock and making for very safe protection.

The first SLCDs on the market came from Wild Country and were four-cam devices called Friends. So popular were they that all SLCDs are now called friends, be they Friends, Camalots, Quadcams, or have any other trade name. Since they were introduced in the 1970s, friends have revolutionized climbing, making protection possible in previously impossible places, and even though they are much more expensive and heavier than wedges, they are a vital part of every climber's equipment.

There are two basic types, steel-stemmed and wire-stemmed. Both are expensive, but the steel-stemmed is slightly cheaper as well as being easier to handle with one hand. The wire-stemmed friend has the advantage that it can be placed where a steel-stemmed might break over a stone edge. A disadvantage is, however, that the strands of the wire can fray and break, one after the other.

Always align the stem with the direction of pull from a fall. It is essential to choose the right size of friend and to place it with care. If it is too big, the cams will not be able to open out enough to provide good contact with the rock and it will be difficult to remove, because you cannot retract the cams enough.

Extracting a friend is often difficult either because it has been wrongly placed or because the leader pulls the climbing rope up too hard, causing the friend to rotate and "walk" back into the crack. Naturally you will not want to leave such an expensive piece of gear on the rock, so it is essential to have a nut key that has two hooks specially for extracting friends.

When using friends

• If the crack is deep, place the piece as close to the edge as possible. Otherwise, it will be difficult to reach the extractor bar when retrieving it. Always check the quality of the rock.
• To be truly safe, all cams must be active and bite into the rock.
• Retract the cams fully before you insert the piece in a crack.
• Keep your friends clean and well lubricated with a silicone-based lubricant.
• When placing a friend, align the stem with the anticipated direction of pull.

PLACING AN SLCD IN A CRACK
The trigger is pulled and the cams are fully retracted before insertion. The stem should point in the direction of pull when the device is inserted in the crack. Be sure to double-check the quality of the surrounding rock.

When the trigger is released inside the crack, the cams open out and bite into the rock on both sides of the crack. The cams should then be half-way retracted. If they are too open or too closed, you should pick a larger or smaller size.

(Above) Wild Country's classic Friend ranges in size from 1 to 4, including half sizes. Size 1, on the left, weighs 91 grams and has a range of 13–19 mm, while the largest Friend, no. 4, on the right, has a range of 64–100 mm and weighs 215 grams.

(Below) Flexible Friends have a stainless steel cable that can bend in all directions. This makes them excellent for placements that are shallow and horizontal.

Equipment

Slings

Woven tape, or webbing, is a versatile item of equipment, being used for runners, slings round flakes and spikes, anchor slings, and quickdraws. The material is synthetic, such as Perlon, Kevlar or Spectra and is available flat or tubular. Flat tape is stronger and stiffer than tubular, which handles better but is also more prone to fraying.

Sewn slings are available in different widths, lengths and colours. The width must suit the size of the carabiner used with the sling. The tape must not fold in on itself in the carabiner. A shock load would concentrate all its power on the fold and the tape could break there.

You can buy tape in suitable lengths and tie your own, using water knots backed up by stopper knots (see page 61), but commercially stitched slings are stronger and neater at the join than knotted ones and this makes them more reliable. Never sew your own slings, it requires special skills and machinery.

Slings are subject to the same wear and tear as your climbing rope, so inspect them regularly and care for them in the same way.

When you buy your first set of slings, remember that you can tie two shorter slings together to make a longer one, so you do not need to buy too many long slings.

For your anchor (for top rope or ground stance), you need at least three slings. One could well be 240 cm (8 ft.) long and 25 mm (1 in.) wide, while the others could be 120 cm (4 ft.) long and 18 mm ($\frac{1}{2}$ in.) or 25 mm (1 in.) wide. They'll be good for girdling tree trunks or stone flakes, or for connecting a friend to the main anchor. Then you need up to a dozen quickdraws, 10–20 cm (4–7 in.) long and 20 mm ($\frac{1}{2}$ in.) wide, as extenders when setting up running belays. Quickdraws have a snaplink carabiner at each end, to ensure speedy clipping in.

Each length and width variant should have its own colour to make it easier for you to distinguish between them on the rock face.

Prusik slings

Prusik slings, which are tied into the climbing rope with Prusik knots (see page 62) are made from 4 metre (13 ft.) lengths of 5 or 6 mm accessory cord. You should always have three Prusik slings with you, two for climbing the rope and one if you need to climb the rope that is tight against an overhang (see pages 106–107). A belayer should also have a Prusik sling in case it is needed to tie off a fallen climber (see pages 46–49).

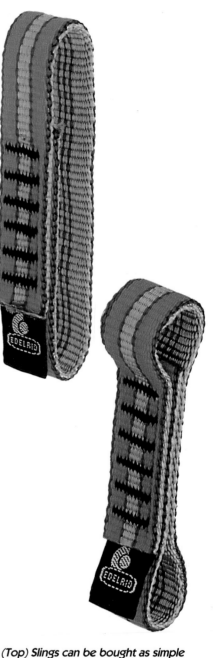

(Top) Slings can be bought as simple lengths which you tie into suitable loops (using a water knot with long tails) or ready-stitched, as 60 cm (24 in.) or 120 cm (48 in.) loops.

(Bottom) Quickdraws, also known as express slings, are available ready made in various sizes. This one is 16 cm (6 in.) long.

A Sticht belay plate from HB Climbing Equipment. Illustrated on the following page is how this type of plate is used.

Belay brakes

A belay brake does *not* automatically arrest and hold a fallen leader. Many beginners make the mistake of thinking that it does. It will only work if the second, who is belaying, handles the rope and the belay brake correctly.

Belay brakes work dynamically, which means that the rope begins to slip if the load passes a certain level. It won't slip much, maybe no more than 40 cm (15 in.), but that is enough to make the arresting action softer on the falling climber.

The Sticht plate

The Sticht plate is highly effective and easy to use and has been widely popular for many years. It is also available with a spring, which increases the dynamic effect and helps prevent the rope from jamming.

It consists of a small metal plate with one slot for a single rope or two slots for a double rope. A short piece of accessory cord ties it to the locking carabiner on the harness tie-on loop, so it is always within reach and cannot be dropped. A bight of the climbing rope is threaded through the hole in the plate and clipped onto the carabiner. When the brake is in use, the braking hand never lets go of the rope.

The tuber

Another belay brake, the tuber has become more and more popular, and if used with care the rope seldom fastens in it, which makes it popular with beginners.

One disadvantage is that it wears out the climbing rope, as it produces a lot of friction.

Other belay brakes

There are many other types of belay brake on the market, for instance the Anka and the Batbrake. These work more or less like the Sticht plate. The ATC brake is another belay brake that is commonly used. It can be seen in function on page 46.

An alternative to a belay plate is to use the small hole of a figure-eight descender, which is normally used to control the speed of an abseil/rappel. Thread a bight of the rope through the small hole of the figure-eight and clip it into a locking carabiner attached to the harness.

The tuber, another kind of belaying device, has become more popular in recent years. On the following page we show how it is used.

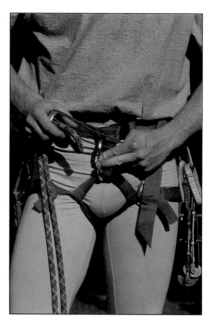

USING A STICHT
A bight of the rope is passed through one of the holes.

The bight is clipped into the locking carabiner on the belayer's waist belt and the carabiner is screwed tight.

The brake hand holds the rope in the locked position. To let some rope out, the belayer moves his hand upwards.

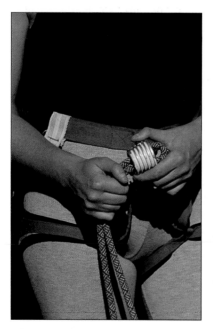

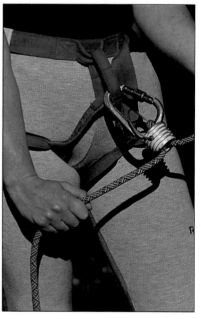

USING A TUBER
The belayer makes a bight of the rope and passes it through the tuber.

She then clips the bight into the locking carabiner on her waist belt and locks the carabiner.

The right hand is the brake hand, while the left hand will hold a controlling grip on the active part of the rope (the part that will run to the climber).

(Above left) The climber has racked up with wedges sorted by size hanging on two carabiners on the gear loop on her left hip.

(Above centre) The gear loop at the back hold her tuber and some friends on slings, while the gear loop at her hip has a number of quickdraws.

(Above right) This climber has added a bandolier with extra gear to complement the rack on his waist belt.

ORGANIZING YOUR GEAR

A well-organized rack contributes to climbing safety. If your chocks, quickdraws, friends and carabiners are haphazardly organized or difficult to get at, you will not be able to find them when you need them, and this can be dangerous. Make a habit of always having your gear hanging in the same order on your rack, so that you can pick out the required piece without even looking.

When you rack up, consistency is the rule. It will save you a lot of time and you will avoid many nervous moments, hanging on with one hand while you desperately search for that No. 8 wedge with the other.

As a beginner, it is tempting to buy a full set of protection gear, but this is not only very expensive, it is also wasteful, as you will certainly not use all of them, or even half, during the first year or so. It is better to buy a basic selection at first and gradually build it up as you notice what is needed. What makes up a suitable rack varies, of course, with the route being climbed, and if you have not climbed it before, check the guide book, ask around, and inspect the route as closely as possible from the ground.

A good choice for a beginner's rack could be:
- *1 long sling (240×25 mm/8 ft.×1in.) with 2 locking carabiners*
- *1 sling (120×18 or 25 mm/4 ft.×3/4 or 1 in.) with 2 snaplink carabiners*
- *6 quickdraws*
- *6 chocks on wire (sizes 3, 5, 6, 7, 9)*
- *2 hexes (sizes 6 and 9)*
- *2 friends (sizes 2 and 3)*
- *3 Prusik slings*
- *4 snaplink carabiners*

Chapter 4

Climbing Techniques

Good climbing technique comes from using your eyes, brain, feet and hands together. These four elements work together to keep you moving up the rock face.

When you climb you use your eyes and brain to decide what you are going to do. They plan your approach to the route as a whole and then they dictate each individual move. When planning a route, remember that you most often get the best overall view on the approach hike to the climb. Guide books and climbers at the rock face who have already climbed the route will often be helpful.

Before you move a hand or foot you must be able to see the hold. Eye contact with the next hold is all-important. The old saying, "Climb with your eyes first", is very true.

Your legs are stronger than your arms, so use your legs and feet more than your arms and hands when you climb. Try not to grip too hard with your hands. Many beginners do this from nerves and in the hope of improving balance, but all they do is tire out their arms and hands. You must conserve energy. Climbing is a sport that can quickly tire the fittest muscles.

On a slab (a rock face with an angle of max 60°) with decent foot holds it is possible to climb with your feet only, using your hands simply to maintain balance. But the more vertical the cliff face, the more important it is to use your hands. A general rule is that the greater reach you make with a foot, the more you need to use your hands. Try to avoid stretching your hands high above your head and keep each foot as directly under its respective hand as possible.

To rest, pick a hold that is as big as possible. Let one limb at a time dangle free and shake it. This will free it from tension and get the blood circulation going.

Climbing Techniques

FOOTWORK

The beginner will instinctively try to stick his toe straight in in a foot hold, which is very tiring on the calf muscles. Better and less tiring support can be obtained, especially from a small foot hold, by using the inside of the foot.

Place your foot with precision on the hold and once there, keep it still. Remember that whenever you move a foot from one hold to the next, the supporting foot must be firmly placed and kept completely still. If you have a decent hand hold, you can lean out a little, which will increase the pressure on your foot, making the foot hold more stable.

Edging

Edging is the technique used when you use the inside of your foot to stand on a small edged foothold. If you have shoes with stiff edges, you will find this technique easier. Get as much shoe edge as possible on the hold. On very small holds, edge with your big toe and keep your heel lower than your toes, to save your calf muscles.

The outside edge of the shoe can also be used for edging, but it will not feel stable. Use of the outer edge of the sole is most common when trying to move to a more secure foot hold. However, when climbing steep overhangs, outside edging is highly efficient as it enables you to keep your centre of gravity over your feet.

Smearing

Smearing is a technique used when the foot hold is very small and is rounded or slopes sharply, making edging impossible. It consists of placing as much of the shoe sole as possible against the hold to obtain enough friction to provide support. Modern "sticky sole" climbing shoes are ideal for smearing as they provide the best friction. The heel is kept low and the ankle rolled outwards to increase contact with the rock.

Try to hold your body as upright as possible, thus increasing foot pressure on the rock. Don't lean in as this will reduce friction and can cause you to lose your footing.

If you are climbing on a slab, you can often obtain friction even on a surface without holds by pointing your toes up the fall line while pressing as much sole as possible to the surface. If your hand holds are stable enough, lean back a little. This will increase your friction and enable you to "walk" up, smoothly shifting your body weight from the one foot to the other.

When climbing on a slab, enough friction can sometimes be obtained by pointing the toes up the fall line and keeping as much of the sole as possible in contact with the rock.

The left foot is in a toe jam (see page 102) while the right foot is smearing on a minute, rounded foot hold. A right-hand jam (see page 101) offers extra stability while the climber examines his next move.

A typical situation where edging with the outside of the shoe is necessary. As soon as the left foot is brought over, the right foot can swivel so that both heels point towards each other.

Edging on a small diagonal crack with the inner right shoe and the outer left. Note the correct position of the heels, well below the toes. This saves the calf muscles from tiring.

A toe-only hold like this is very tiring and should be moved from as quickly as possible. Again, note the low heel position.

HAND HOLDS

A hand hold is any kind of protuberance or hollow in the rock, from a solid shelf edge to a small crack, where you can get a supporting grip.

If the hold is large and rounded, you can use the *open grip*, i.e., you use your whole hand (palm, fingers and thumb). Pressing the palm to the hold increases friction.

A tiny ledge that you can get your finger tips on provides a *cling grip*. This is not particularly stable but if there is space to get your thumb up beside your fingers, it will help. The best thing is to get your thumb over the top of your index finger and press down on it. This stabilizes the grip somewhat and also distributes the load more evenly over the tendons.

If the hold is a "jug", i.e., positive with room enough for you to curve your hand round it, using your combined fingers as a hook, the grip is known as a *vertical grip*.

The *pinch grip* enables you to press two surfaces towards each other. If the hold is very small, for instance a protuberance the size of a pebble, you can pinch it between thumb and forefinger. If it is large, pinch it between your thumb and all your fingers.

(Top left) The open grip, for a large, rounded hold. Press the palm to the hold to increase friction.

(Top right) The cling grip give the finger tops purchase on tiny cracks.

(Centre left) The vertical grip, also known as a jug or hook grip, is a stable hand grip.

(Centre right) The pinch grip, also known as the squeeze grip, entails squeezing two surfaces towards each other.

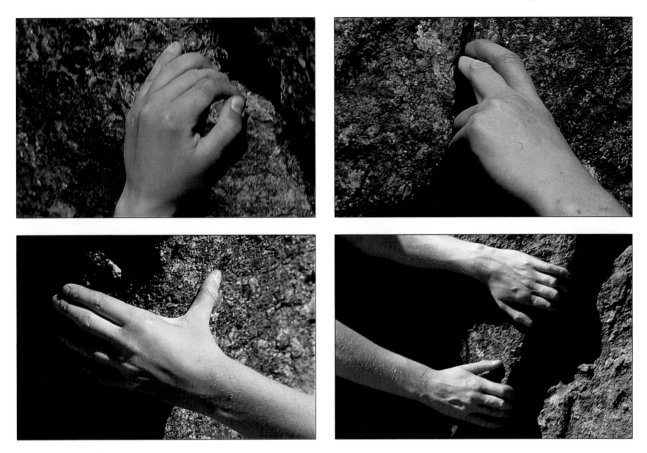

(Top left) The finger wrap grip gets the maximum contact between fingers and the surface of a rock knob.

(Top right) The finger grip inserts one or two fingers into a tiny crack or pocket in the rock. Twisting the finger(s) produces a camming effect.

(Centre left) A large pinch grip can extend the hand fully. Press the palm against the rock for greater friction.

(Centre right) A side pull with one or two hands gives support on a vertical or diagonal flake.

The *finger wrap* is a combination of the cling and pinch grips. The hold is a large pebble, or knob, and you wrap as many fingers as there is room for round it, with your little finger against the cliff face. Stabilize this grip by pressing your thumb against your index finger (or whichever finger is farthest out in the wrap).

The *finger grip* involves inserting one or two fingers into a small pocket. Flatten your palm against the rock to increase friction. Then twist your hand clockwise slightly to improve the grip. If you can get two fingers into the pocket, all the better.

If the pocket is higher than it is wide, you can place one finger on top of the other to make the grip stronger.

The *side pull* is used if the hand hold is a vertical or diagonal flake. The climber pulls out on the hold in order to find the necessary support. The side pull is also used when laybacking.

* * *

A cliff face will, of course, provide many variations on these hand holds, and you will often have to provide your own variant in order to solve an unusual hold.

BALANCE AND RHYTHM

Rock climbing is a dynamic sport that demands balance and smooth, rhythmic progress. Good balance means that your centre of gravity is squarely over your feet. As you climb your centre of gravity will be constantly shifting, but you must keep it over your feet. For instance, if you are standing on both feet on a narrow ledge and shift all your weight onto one foot, you must move your body so that its centre of gravity is over the supporting foot.

The nearer the rock your centre of gravity moves, the less you are straining your fingers. That is not to say that you must be pressed up against the rock. In fact, a typical beginner's mistake is a posture in which head and shoulders are leaning in too much while the behind is sticking out. This moves the centre of gravity away from where it should be and increases the strain on the fingers. This can often lead to joint and/or tendon injury, especially when the climber is untrained. Another problem with this posture is that it is practically impossible to see the next hand or foot hold when your head is too close to the rock.

Correct body posture is therefore important. Hold your body upright, with its centre of gravity squarely over your feet, and with enough space between body and rock to allow the next holds to be seen and the feet to be lifted.

Plan short, smooth moves

Always try to make smooth, economical progress from one position to the next. Each move should be the result of a conscious

(Left) The climber has deliberately got into this position to demonstrate vividly what bad balance can do. Because his centre of gravity is not over his feet he is going to have to use arm strength and some nifty footwork to get himself into a good position again.

(Right) Back to a proper balance position, his centre of gravity is well centred over his feet and he can rest a little while planning his next move.

Short, smooth moves, like the sequence shown above (left to right), linked together encourage the development of a good climbing rhythm that moves you up the rock face at a suitable pace.

decision and planned in advance. Planning in advance will mean that you use the least amount of energy needed for the move.

Also, keep your moves short. They will be less strenuous, allow more control and enable you to maintain good balance, and when you have finished one move you will be in the correct starting position for the next.

If possible, choose hand holds that are at shoulder or head height. Stretching above your head again and again is tiring, and if you find a hold above your head, the natural tendency is to lean the upper body in to the rock, with the aforementioned results.

If it is difficult to find a suitable hold, remember to look to your side and even down to the left and right. It is quite possible that you will see a hold that you can push down on to enable you to get into a better position for your next move.

When you find a hand hold and place your hand on it, check it first to see if it feels comfortable and if it will hold for the pressure you are going to subject it to. Then if you are satisfied with your choice, place your hand firmly in the hold and look to where you have planned your next foot hold.

If you discover that the move is not working, retrace your steps and think again. What alternatives are available? Make a new decision and off you go again. Keep your three points of contact with the rock as still as possible while you move your fourth limb, and remember not to pull yourself up with your hands but to push yourself up with your legs.

MANTLING

Mantling is used when you come to a shelf or a large foot hold. Successful mantling requires strength and good coordination.

If the shelf is not above chest height, place the palms of your hands on it with your fingertips pointing at each other. Launch yourself with your feet, taking very small steps up the rock face at the same time as you push down on your hands. When high enough, lean your body, arms cocked, in so that your weight is over your hands. In this position you can grab a moment's rest before straightening your arms and lifting up one foot onto the shelf beside your hands. Find a higher hand hold and then lift the other foot up and stand up on the shelf.

If the shelf is too high for this method, you have a more difficult move to make. Feel around on the shelf until you find good holds. Check that there is room beside your hands for the foot that will

MANTLING ONTO A SMALL SHELF
(Top left) A jug grip allows you to lean back and work your feet up until . . .

(Top centre) . . . your chest is passing your hands and you can cock your elbows and lean in a little.

(Top right) Swivel your hands so that the fingers point at each other. Push up with feet and hands.

(Lower left) One hand on the ledge, the other reaches for a grip. Lift one foot onto the shelf.

(Lower centre) Bring the other foot up, steady with one hand on the shelf and side-pull with the other.

Then move the side pull higher up and stand up, reaching for a new grip with your left hand.

MANTLING ONTO A WIDE SHELF
This shelf is just above chest height, so the palms cannot be placed on it with the fingers pointing towards each other, as described opposite. A version of this method works fine, however.

(Top left) Place the palms on the shelf and prepare to push up with your feet and pull up with your hands and arms.

(Top centre) Halfway there, with straight arms, the upper body tilted inwards over the edge of the shelf and the toes getting the best purchase they can.

(Top right) One foot is lifted up between the hands, the body leans further in over the shelf.

(Centre left) The other foot is now lifted up onto the shelf. Good balance is kept by the other limbs steadying and supporting the upper body.

(Centre right) Well mantled! Mantling demands commitment and will. Practise mantling whenever possible.

be brought up first. Otherwise you'll be in the embarrassing and dangerous position of standing on your own hand in the middle of a power move! Lean back slightly to give your feet room to move and launch yourself boldly up, taking quick, short, friction-making foot holds to bring the upper part of your body over your hands. As your chest passes your hands, swivel them so the fingers point at each other and cock your arms so that they are pushing down instead of pulling up. Then straighten your arms and lift one foot onto the ledge. Rest a second as this is a very tiring move. Find a hand hold a bit higher up and then bring up the other foot and stand up on the shelf.

Needless to say, this technique needs a lot of practice. Try to find a couple of different mantelshelves on a bouldering rock, where you can safely practise. A ground-floor stone window shelf will also do nicely for training mantling.

COUNTERFORCES

Forces that work in opposing directions can be exploited to create friction and enhance balance and support. If you push down with one hand on a hold at below hip level at the same time as you push up with the other hand on the underside of an overhang you will produce a counterforce that will provide plenty of support while you work out your next move. The following three techniques, *laybacking*, *bridging* and *undercling* are all based on the use of counterforces.

(Top left) "Opening" a crack.

(Top centre) Using a thumb to oppose fingers in a crack.

(Top right) Counterforcing with the feet.

(Lower left) A giant pinch grip is a counterforce grip.

(Lower centre) Stemming with the feet gives a counterforce.

(Lower right) As does stemming with the hands.

(Top left) The arms are crossed and side-pulling.

(Top right) The right arm moves above the left and the climber leans back, legs bent.

(Centre left) The left hand has moved up and the legs push up.

(Centre right) The left hand has moved up again. That straight right leg is OK here because the left foot supports. If both feet are on the same surface, the knees must be kept bent.

Beginners often forget to keep their legs bent, and this puts too much pressure on the hands and arms.

Laybacking

Also known as liebacking, this strenuous technique is used when climbing an arête or if a vertical or diagonal crack offers good side pull while there is room for your feet to push in the opposite direction. Keeping your arms as straight as possible to reduce muscle strain, lean back while walking your feet, one at a time, up towards your hands. The closer your feet get to your hands, the more unstable your position, but it is important you get them as close as possible so that the pull is countering the push. When you are in the layback position, with straight arms and bent (not straight) legs, move the top hand up and follow it with the other hand. Then move the upper foot up and follow it with the other. Continue shuffling up in this way, a little at a time. Keep your heels as close to the rock as possible to avoid slipping. Use your outer leg to keep your body pressed in towards the rock to avoid swinging out in the so-called "barndoor effect".

(Left) Climbing a corner by bridging up the opposing walls. The soles of shoes are as flat as possible against the rock surfaces to obtain maximum friction. This method is not strenuous and the arms can be rested regularly while the feet maintain the bridge.

(Right) The left hand pushes down and the right hand steadies, preparatory to one foot being lifted to a new position.

Bridging

Bridging, or stemming, as it is also called, is the best way to handle a gap or a corner. You can also bridge when you want to exploit two parallel cracks to make upward progress.

Once in the corner, you push one foot against the one wall and the other foot against the other. Lean the body slightly into the corner using your hands mainly to keep balance but also to increase the counterforce when moving a foot. Upward progress is made in short moves, one foot at a time. Just before you move a foot you brace yourself with both hands and stand as much as possible with your weight over the support foot.

Bridging is not strenuous. Your weight is mainly on your feet, so a bridging position can even be used to rest, as it allows the climber to stand securely, free to rest and shake out the arms.

In the undercling position you can rest for a while while considering what to do.

The undercling movement, however, is a transitional, dynamic moving of the body from a position where counterforces are in action (the arms pulling up and the feet pressing down), often past a slight overhang, to a new position from where the climber can continue up the rock face.

(Left) Pressing down with the feet and pulling up with the hands in the undercling movement, the climber keeps his body out from the rock to put most of the pressure on his legs and feet, increasing the friction between the soles of his shoes and the rock.

(Right) Keeping his eyes on his feet, he works them up the rock to a new position. His next move, which follows without stopping, will be to reach out with one hand for a grip higher up.

Undercling

The undercling is yet another push-pull technique that is very useful for giving yourself a rest or when you want to make a long reach for a high hand hold. The best underclings are at hip level and you grip them with your palms up, pulling up while you push down with your feet.

Climbing Techniques

Switching feet or hands

In many climbing situations, for instance when progressing along a horizontal crack (traversing), you are going to find that reaching your next foot/hand hold is going to entail switching feet/hands. The three-point contact with the rock rule may have to be waived here for a split second, so it is vital that you know where that fourth limb is going to end up, should the third not make it into position.

You are, for instance, standing on a small knob with your weight mainly on your left foot, which makes it easy for you to lead with your right foot. However, the next foot hold is best reached with your left foot. If you go for it with your right, your centre of gravity will shift and you will lose balance. Therefore, you must switch feet.

A dynamic foot switch can be risky, especially if your hand holds are not solid. Basically, it consists of a little hop up so that the supporting foot leaves the knob at the same time as you whip the other foot into its place. Lean out a little, using your hand holds to support you while you are hopping. Good coordination is important here.

A static foot switch is safer, but to be able to carry it out you must find some room on the hold for your non-supporting foot. Stand with the supporting foot on the hold and squeeze the toe of your other foot in beside it. Take your weight on your hands while you work the non-supporting foot onto the hold and ease the other one off it.

The same problem arises (and the same solution applies) when you want to switch hands. Remember that you must know where the next hand hold is for the hand that you are about to slide out of the hold when the new hand comes in.

THE DYNAMIC FOOT SWITCH
(Opposite, left) The starting position. Standing on his left foot, the climber wants to get his right foot on to the foothold. Watching very closely where his feet are, the climber prepares to make a small hop.

(Opposite, top right) Putting all his weight on his hands, he compresses his body and takes a short, explosive hop. . .

(Opposite, centre right). . . that lifts his left foot from the hold, so that he can whip his right foot onto it.

(Opposite, bottom right) The switch complete, the climber can now move his left foot to its new hold.

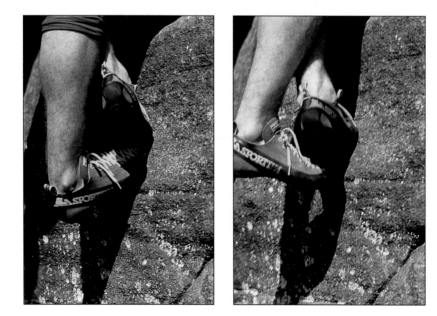

THE STATIC FOOT SWITCH
(Left) The right foot has a tiny hold onto which the climber wants to move the left foot.

(Centre) While taking as much weight as possible on his hands, the climber works in his left foot from above, while he withdraws the right.

CRACK CLIMBING

Cracks in the rock are a natural part of many cliffs and present the climber with a challenging problem which may be insoluble if he does not learn about jamming. Routes very often follow cracks, especially on smooth cliffs that offer no other way up, and provide a wide variety of interesting hand and foot holds. Crack climbing requires precision and a creative approach, as well as the will to solve the problems that are sure to arise. Many climbers regard jamming as the skill that makes or breaks a climber.

When the cracks are such that you cannot use them as normal hand and foot holds, you must gain purchase by jamming in your finger(s), hand or fist and knees, toes or feet, depending on the size of the crack. It is strenuous, it hurts and it produces many scrapes and scars. And it is often the only way to climb a route.

Finger and hand jamming

The *finger jam* is for cracks so thin that only one or at most all your fingers can fit. It is most secure if you can get your finger(s) in up to the knuckle. Your thumb should point down and the palm and other fingers spread on the rock surface to increase friction – this will lock the hand in position.

Some cracks are so small that only the little finger can fit. The thumb should point up and, again, twisting the hand until the palm spreads on the rock will give this jam a little more stability. The *little-finger*, or *pinkie*, *jam* is still fairly unstable, however.

If you can get several fingers into the crack up as far as your knuckles you can twist your hand and create a *finger lock*. The resulting jam is considerably more stable than the little-finger jam. If you can press your thumb against the rock to the side of the crack, the counterforce produced makes for an even better jam.

A third variation of the finger jam is if the crack narrows in the middle and then flares out again. Stick your index or long finger into the crack above the narrow part and your thumb into the crack below. Pinch together and you have an effective *ring jam*.

The *hand jam* is used when you can get your whole hand into the crack. Keep it flat when inserting it and then bend your fingers, folding the thumb into the palm. If this is not possible, place the thumb on top of the index finger's lowest joint and press down to stabilize the jam. Rotate your wrist a little to cam the hand in the crack. Not comfortable, but if your hand is too loose in the crack, you can get pretty severe abrasions. Create a counterforce by pressing the fingertips against one side of the crack while pressing the back of your hand against the other side.

A finger jam. Getting the thumb in as well increases the grip's stability.

A finger lock is a finger jam which is cammed by twisting the hand. Press the palm against the rock.

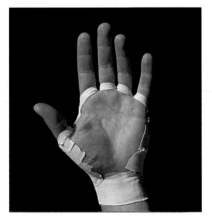

Jamming, specially when you rotate your wrist to cam your hand, is painful and will cause scrapes and sores. Taping the hand helps (palm view).

The little-finger, or pinkie, jam.

The finger jam. Rotating the hand cams the jam and the palm against the rock increases the stability of the jam.

The boxing-fist jam. Press the thumb down on the index finger.

The thumb-in-palm fist jam, with the hand "face on", provides a jam in a wider crack.

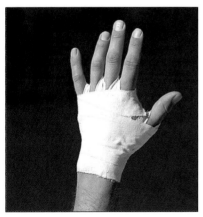

The same hand as opposite, now seen from the other side. Some even tape their fingers between the joints.

The hand jam. Pressing with the thumb against one side and the back of the hand against the other stabilizes the jam.

The thumb-in-palm hand jam gives a broader jam.

Climbing Techniques

The *fist jam* is used when the crack is too big for a hand jam. This works best in a crack that tapers somewhat. Insert your hand and clench it into a fist, with the thumb either tucked into your palm or lying pressed down on top of the second joint of your index finger, like a boxer's fist.

Foot jamming

Foot holds are important when you are hand jamming, so that you can relieve the pressure on your hands now and then. If there are no holds to the side of the crack it may be possible to jam your foot, or maybe both, into the crack down below your hands. Twist your foot to one side and insert the toe in the crack, preferably just over where it tapers. Twist the foot back to the normal position so that the sides of the crack are pressing against the sides of your climbing shoe's toe. Lower your heel. This is the *toe jam*.

If the crack is too big for a toe jam and you manage to get in your whole foot, press the heel against one side of the crack and your toe against the other. This is the *foot jam*, also known as the *heel-toe jam*, and is a good stable jam which will even allow you to rest.

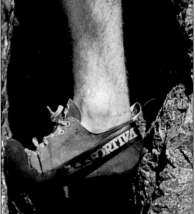

(Top) The toe jam. Insert the toe with your foot twisted sideways and then return the foot to normal, creating a camming effect.

(Centre) The foot jam, or heel-toe jam.

(Left) Foot stacking is used when the crack is too wide for a foot jam, so you jam in both feet, often one just above the other, to obtain a solid jam.

OFF-WIDTH JAMS

Both the shots on this page were taken on a hot, bright day. Normally, the climber would wear a long-armed shirt of tough material to protect his skin from abrasion!

In a narrow off-width crack, you use your entire arm to create a jam. This is known as an arm bar. The back of the upper arm pushes against one side of the off-width, while the palm of the hand pushes against the other.

In a wide off-width, the arm is bent so that you can insert it elbow first. When you press your palm against one side , the back of your upper arm is automatically pressed against the other side.

Off-width

A crack that is too wide for a fist jam but not wide enough to take the whole body is called off-width. Climbing off-width is a demanding technique that entails jamming the whole arm or the whole leg, where possible using counterforces. You can, for instance, jam your arm into a crack and exert pressure on one side of the crack with the back of your upper arm and your shoulder while pressing on the other side with the palm of your hand. This is known as the *arm bar*. If possible, you get your leg into the same crack lower down, and when you have found purchase with this *leg lock*, you use the limbs that are outside the crack to find holds that will lift you up. For instance, you can push down on a knob or other suitable point with your free foot or hand.

Off-width climbing is tough on joints and skin, so don't wear singlet and shorts if you off-width . . .

Chimneying

If you can get your whole body into the crack, which is then known as a chimney, you create counterforces by pressing with your back and hands against one side of the chimney and with the soles of your feet against the other side. In other words, this is a body jam that allows you to adopt a good resting position any time.

Your size and height can be a problem if you are following a leader who is considerably taller/shorter/fatter/thinner than you are, as what suits them perfectly may be impossible for you!

You progress up the chimney by moving one foot (say the left) from the facing wall and, bending the knee, you press the sole against the opposite wall, underneath your behind. Put your right hand on the facing wall and push up with your left hand, which is at waist height, and left foot, at the same time as you push up with your right foot. Your right hand is used mainly to steady yourself and maintain balance. When you are back in the rest position, you switch feet and continue.

If the chimney is narrow, you may have to use your knees on the facing wall, with both your feet under you. This is a much harder variant, and knee pads are recommended.

IN A WIDE CHIMNEY
(Left) Working the feet up one by one, and creating counterforce by pushing against opposing walls with the hands. More counterforce is created by pressing the feet against one wall and the back against the other.

(Right) In this position, the climber can rest before continuing up the chimney.

IN A NARROW CHIMNEY

Narrow chimneys are also known, for obvious reasons, as squeeze chimneys.

(Top left) The climber has cammed his body into this narrow chimney, hands pushing at opposing sides, and his feet pushing his back against the other side.

(Top centre) He reaches up for a hand hold above his head, stretching his body while pushing up with his feet and with his other hand.

(Top right) Now fully erect, he has got a good grip on that high hold and, pulling and pushing with his hands, he works his feet up until . . .

(Centre left) . . . his body is jack-knifed securely while he figures out his next move which . . .

(Centre right) . . . he now launches into, using his feet and outer hand to push himself up for another high reach.

There are usually plenty of holds in a chimney, which makes it a reasonably easy way to climb a section of a route without too much effort. Beginners are often tempted to move into the very back of the chimney, as it feels safer there. Avoid this, because it is usually more cramped there and because there are often better hand holds at the outer edges.

Climbing Techniques

ROPE CLIMBING

If an emergency arises, you may need to climb up or down the rope, for example to reach your partner who has got into difficulties and needs your help or if you cannot continue climbing due to weather or failing light.

Rope-climbing techniques must be practised. Being able to climb the rope may save your life in a tricky situation. If there is a big tree in the garden you can hang a rope from a high, sturdy branch and practise there in safety. Or if you have a first-floor balcony, hang a rope from the railing and practise there.

You can use mechanical aids, such as Jumars, for climbing a rope, but the Prusik technique is recommended because you do not need to bring any extra hardware along, just a few Prusik slings. Also, if you have to climb an abseil/rappel rope, the Prusik method is absolutely the best, because the Jumar will not hold on two ropes.

Prusiking

Make two Prusik slings from suitable lengths of 4-mm kernmantle accessory cord. The lengths are given approximately here, because Prusik slings must be tied to suit each individual climber's arm and leg lengths. Once the slings are measured and tied, they should be kept that way, as you don't want to have to measure and tie the slings in an emergency on the rock face. One (about 50 cm/20 in. long) will run from your harness and be tied with a Prusik knot to the climbing rope at about head level. It must not be so long that the knot can get out of reach. The other sling (about 1 metre/3 ft. long) runs from one foot and is also tied to the rope with a Prusik knot. The foot sling is always tied to the rope below the harness sling.

Prusiking entails standing in the foot sling to lock the Prusik knot and to take the full weight of the body. The harness sling, which is now free of tension, can be pushed an arm's length up the rope. Now sit down in your harness so that your weight shifts from the foot sling to the harness sling, which will lock as the tension increases and allow you to hang comfortably in the harness, while you move up the foot sling so that its knot is as close as possible to the harness sling's knot. Repeat the procedure until you have reached your goal.

When you stand up in the foot sling, keep the lower part of your body close to the climbing rope, while the upper body can lean out a little to allow you to see where you are going. If the climbing rope is in contact with an abrasive edge, lean back more to lift the rope off the edge. If you need to steady yourself, you can place one foot on the rock face.

If you come to an overhang where the rope is tight against the rock, it will be difficult to move the harness sling's knot past the edge of the overhang. Press your body out from the rock with

PRUSIKING

(Opposite) The climber needs to climb up the climbing rope, so he uses the Prusik method. He ties two Prusik slings to the rope: the green-and-yellow foot sling and the red-and-blue harness sling.

When he sits down in his harness, the sling's Prusik knot tightens on the rope while the foot sling's Prusik knot is unweighted. The harness sling supports him fully while he slides the foot sling's Prusik knot up or down the rope.

When he stands again, the foot sling's Prusik knot tightens and the foot sling holds his weight while he slides the harness-sling's knot along the rope, and in this way he progresses up or down the rope.

Sitting down in his harness, the climber slides the Prusik knot on the foot sling up along the rope.

He now stands up and slides the harness sling's knot up the rope (but not out of reach when he sits down again).

Sitting down again, he checks carefully that the Prusik knot on the harness sling is actually holding properly, before ...

. . . again moving the foot sling's knot up the rope, as close as possible to the other Prusik knot.

This sequence is repeated. Note how the climber keeps the lower part of his body close to the rope.

As a final picture in this sequence, we show him resting in his harness, steadying himself against the rock face with his free foot.

ONE-SLING PRUSIKING
This kind of Prusiking requires only one Prusik sling but is only safe for climbing up the rope, not down.

(Above left) A red-and-yellow Prusik sling connects the harness to the climbing rope.

(Above centre) He loops the climbing rope round his foot as shown, so that when he stands in it, it will hold his weight without slipping.

(Above right) Standing in the rope loop he holds the climbing rope tight in one hand, steadying himself on the active rope with other hand.

(Far left) He slides the Prusik knot up the rope.

(Left) He sits down in his harness and lifts his foot up, rearranges the loop round it, and prepares to raise himself up again on the foot in the rope loop.

your free foot, so that there is room enough between the rope and the rock to slide the knot past the edge. If that doesn't work, tie another Prusik sling from your harness to the rope above the overhang, let it take the tension and then carry on. That third Prusik sling is necessary, not just for this situation, but also for when you need to escape from the system.

As a precaution against the Prusik knots not locking on the rope, tie every fifth metre/yard or so of the rope that you have climbed to your harness. This means that you will only slide back about 5 metres (16 ft.) if the Prusik knot doesn't hold. Even when they are under tension, Prusik knots *can* glide on the rope, as they must be loose enough to glide and hard enough to lock tight under tension. Another risk is that heavy friction can cause the knot to melt.

ANOTHER ROPE-CLIMBING METHOD
A ratchet device attached to a locking carabiner on the harness serves instead of a harness Prusik.

The climber sits down in his harness, and the ratchet locks on the rope.

Standing up in the Prusik loop, the climber slides the ratchet device up the rope.

He can now sit down again, allowing the ratchet device to take his weight.

He lifts the unweighted Prusik knot up the rope, close to the ratchet device.

Standing up again, the Prusik tightens and takes his weight. Note how the lower body is kept close to the rope.

Chapter 5
Training

*The best way to improve your climbing is –
to climb! But training will also help you
improve your performance.*

The more you climb the better you will become, but not all of us can climb throughout the year. However, indoor climbing walls are being set up all over and you can use these during the off-season to keep in good physical trim and to improve the weak points in your climbing technique.

Climbing is a demanding sport – it makes greater physical demands on its devotees than do most other sports. The active climber must be reasonably strong and flexible, and must have good physical and mental endurance. This means that training for climbing must be planned so that it helps to improve all these different elements.

As already pointed out, buying first-class gear is not enough to make you a good climber. You need to know how to use it. You must also have mastered the basic techniques and understand the ethics involved. (These are best acquired through a course with an officially recognized climbing club.) And then you need to have a good standard of basic fitness.

Basic fitness (cardio-vascular fitness) is easily developed by regular physical activities such as jogging, swimming, ballgames of all sorts, cycling and workouts. In fact, any activity that you do regularly, makes you breathless and brings out a good sweat will improve your cardio-vascular fitness. And apart from making you fitter, this kind of training helps get rid of that extra blubber you are carrying. Losing unnecessary weight will make your climbing easier, but note the word "unnecessary". Do not think that starving will make you a better climber.

Power and stamina training in your local gym will also improve your climbing performance. Many climbers install pull-up bars or boards in their homes. These are fine for developing

specific muscle groups, but too much pull-up training can have an adverse effect. You must train *all* your muscles.

Warming up

It is always risky to skip warming up before physical exercise. For instance, if you have a pull-up board in the hallway at home and you make a habit of doing a few pull-ups every time you pass, you can actually damage some muscles or sinews, just because they were not warmed up.

It is impossible to measure how much a proper warming-up session will improve your climbing performance, but the fact that it certainly diminishes the risk for straining or even rupturing a muscle should be sufficient reason for you never to miss out. This applies before both climbing and training sessions. In other words, you should warm up before every kind of strenuous physical activity.

You often see people stretching before they start training or climbing. They are stretching "cold", and many of those involved in sports medicine say that this is dangerous. There is, however, another school that in recent years claims this is not so. Until they work out what is what, you are going to have to decide for yourself. Do what feels best, is our advice.

Normal body temperature lies at around 37°C (98.6°F). Inside

PREPARING TO CLIMB
Before you start a day's climbing it is important to warm up. The hike in to the foot of the cliff may have got your body temperature up nicely, but an inactive ten minutes, getting your climbing clothes on and getting your gear sorted out or waiting for the route to be free, is enough to cool you down again. There are lots of ways of warming up, and some of them are described here. Stretching is another important part of your pre-climb preparations.

(Above) Two climbers hang from a low branch, an exercise that has a two-fold benefit: it raises body temperature and stretches the ligaments and muscles in the limbs, thus lubricating the joints of the fingers, hands, arms, legs, hips and shoulders.

ANOTHER STRETCHING EXERCISE
Use whatever natural aid you can find at the foot of the cliff to stretch. This low branch is perfect for stretching the muscles in the backs of your arms and legs and in your shoulders. Hanging from the branch by your hands and then your fingers will loosen up and lubricate the joints in the hands and fingers nicely.

Get into the habit of doing the same warming-up and stretching exercises before every climb. Make it a regular part of your pre-climb routine. It is an important safety factor and will save you from damaging muscles.

a muscle the temperature can vary from 35 to 39°C (96 to 102°F), depending on whether it is highly active or totally inactive. A muscle with a temperature of just 35°C (96°F) will react a bit more slowly than if it were warm, and it will have greater difficulty in producing the explosive power necessary for a particularly hard move.

The best way to warm up the complete system is to jog for ten to fifteen minutes. There may be no jogging trail near the rock but you can always jog in place with extra-high knees, mixed with hopping and back kicks. A brisk thirty-minute march to the beginning of the route, especially if you are carrying your equipment with you, will give the same increase in muscle temperature and will also get the joints "well-oiled".

The problem with climbing is that it is a stop-start sport. Setting up an anchor and getting the gear in order takes time, which will cool you down. Belaying a leader takes more mental than physical energy, so you can be quite cold when it is your turn to climb. Remember this and do all you can to keep muscle temperature up.

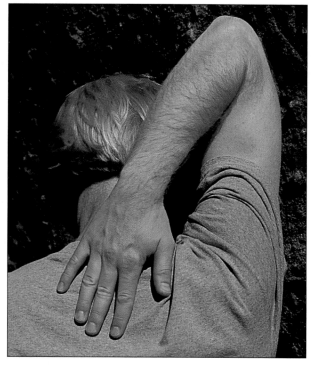

MORE STRETCHING EXERCISES
*(Above) Reach as far down your back you can.
Stretches the muscles of the upper arm.*

*(Left) This stretches the Achilles' tendon in the ankle.
Do it slowly.*

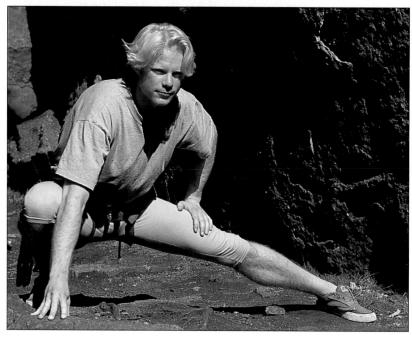

*(Above) Loosen up the fingers and
lubricate the joints by pressing
them against a surface. Don't forget
to do the same thing with your
thumbs.*

*(Left) This is a good exercise for
stretching the muscles on the inside
of your thigh and your knee.*

Bouldering

Bouldering is low-level climbing without protection. You climb on "mini-walls", big boulders and such. It means that you can jump down without injuring yourself, anytime you want.

In many countries, bouldering has developed into a sport in its own right and some people have gone in for it wholeheartedly. For the ordinary rock climber it is unbeatable as a method of training balance and technique, and it is an excellent way for the beginner to learn basic hand- and footwork without having to set up anchors and so on. When you boulder, you are not hindered by heavy gear that restricts your freedom of movement. All you have is your chalk bag, so you can concentrate fully on the boulder and the special problems that it presents. Each boulder will have its own characteristics, each a new problem that has to be solved with a combination of hands, feet, eyes and brain.

You won't have to travel far to find a suitable boulder, and all the equipment you need is a pair of shoes and that chalk bag. Even if bouldering is the only form of climbing that can sensibly be done solo, it is definitely safest, and more fun, if you have a climbing partner with you. You may not have far to fall, but there is always a risk of twisting an ankle when you drop off the boulder. Your partner stands below you and supports you as you land (this is called spotting). And apart from the feeling of security that a companion can give, he can also give encouragement and advice, and you can talk through the various problems that arise. And when you manage to solve a particularly difficult problem, you will spur your partner to better you. There is nothing like a bit of competition!

Try to find a boulder with different crack sizes, different kinds of holds, ledges and pockets. This is what you will find when you lead regular routes. Try climbing in all directions: up, down, sideways and diagonally. It is often said that a 100 metres/yards covered lead climbing is equal to one hour's bouldering, from the point of view of what you can learn.

So what can you learn from bouldering? Balance is a major element of your technique that will improve with bouldering. Some people are born with a good sense of balance, others not. It is easier to check how good your balance is, when you know that you have a drop of only a metre or two below you! Balance is best improved by concentrating on climbing with your feet only. Daring moves can also be attempted, and success at these will build up your climbing confidence.

Bouldering will thus improve your basic techniques and teach you to choose the best holds for your hands and feet. As a beginner you will soon notice the difference in strength between hands and feet, already referred to. The more you use your feet the less quickly you will tire.

When you go bouldering, practise placing your feet: edging, smearing, front-on. Notice how leaning out from the rock a little will increase friction between your shoe sole and the rock. Practise holding an upright position, with your weight square over your feet. A common beginner's error already referred to is to stick your behind out, but if you do this, your centre of gravity will be wrong, and your hands will have to take most of the strain.

General fitness will give you the strength to climb the first part of a pitch, but endurance will give you the staying power to complete it.

Endurance is a very important attribute in the climber's physical makeup, and it is easy to forget to work on this when you are bouldering, because the "pitches" in bouldering are so short. Simulate longer pitches by working sideways and forwards and backwards several times without taking a break.

When you have been bouldering a while you will begin to realize the importance of physical and mental agility. You learn to think quickly and to translate your thoughts into actions that are carried out in smooth, rhythmic movements that will not tire you out as quickly as jerky bursts of energy would.

BOULDERING

Bouldering is the best kind of training for the rock climber. Unencumbered by a harness and a rack of gear, you can practise all-round climbing technique or specific areas that you feel need improving.

Bouldering develops strength, coordination and agility (mental and physical). It also trains you to visualize climbing moves in a sequence.

(Above left) Foot jamming up a diagonal crack using hand holds to keep balance. Note the posture, which keeps the weight centred over the feet.

(Above right) Practising the use of minimal foot holds while making a long reach.

BUILDERING

Urbanized bouldering, "buildering" is an increasingly popular training method for those who cannot regularly get near a real cliff face. So popular has this kind of climbing become that some keen builderers are writing guide books for their favourite city sites!

Here, the wall of an old fortification is used for practice, but any big wall, or a stone-built church or even a bridge will provide excellent buildering surfaces. It is wise to obtain permission from the appropriate quarter first . . .

(Above left) The mortared joins between the stones provide a wide variety of hand holds. The left hand has a solid, open hold to support the tiny cling grip that the right hand has.

(Above right) This outer corner of the fortification is in effect an arête. As negotiating an arête often subjects the climber to a lot of exposure, it is a good idea to practise it at low level before taking it on on a real rock face.

(Right) Suitable buildering sites can provide the whole spectrum of climbing situations. Two walls of this fortification are built inward to join and form a dieder that is perfect for training bridging, or stemming as it is also called.

A TRAINING SCHEDULE

Beginners always feel that lack of strength and endurance is one of their major weaknesses, especially when they compare themselves to those who have been climbing regularly for a season or more. Aches and pains indicate the presence of muscles that they never even knew existed.

You can increase your strength and endurance by training (see below) but there is another element of physical fitness that is important for the climber, namely flexibility. That too can be improved by systematic training. The following training schedule takes these three aspects of physical fitness into account. Reach good level of fitness in all three and you will soon notice an improvement in your climbing.

Muscles

You are born with a certain number of muscle fibres in each cell. Training will make each fibre and consequently each muscle larger and therefore stronger.

There are two types of muscle fibres, slow and fast. The slow fibres control endurance and the fast fibres control how much explosive strength you have. When you train with light weights, many repeats and at slow speed only the slow fibres work and, therefore, develop.

The fast muscle fibres reach full power in about half the time it takes the slow to do the same. To develop the fast muscle fibres, you must work with heavy weights or repeat an exercise so many times that the last few reps feel really strenuous.

To give your muscles the best all-round training you must vary the weights and the speeds you work at. If you never go for maximum effort, you are not going to develop the whole muscle. Intensive training with heavy weights will give you strong back muscles and weak chest muscles. If you don't vary your training, for instance do only pull-ups, then your muscles fibres will be short, which means that you will be strong but lack flexibility.

Training for max strength

A normal training session to increase maximum strength is three sets of six reps each with weights that are 80% of what you can lift when you are exerting yourself fully. Let's suppose that 25 kg (60 lbs) is the maximum that you can lift. You should train with weights that are 80% of that, i.e. 20 kg (48 lbs). So you lift 20 kg (48 lbs) six times and take a short break. Do this three times.

After a number of sessions like this, spread out over a few weeks, you might be able to lift 30 kg (70 lbs). Then you train with 24 kg (56 lbs) weights, and three sets of six reps, as above.

INCREASING MUSCLE STRENGTH

In the beginning the safest approach to strength training is to use your body weight to load your muscles. Later, you can start weight training, but always do it under guidance until you have learnt the technique and how much weight you should handle. Otherwise you can very easily cause yourself an injury.

The classic push-up strengthens the chest muscles, the triceps (back of the upper arm) and the flexors (lower arm) as well as the shoulders. The closer together the hands are, the more the flexors in the lower arm must work. The further apart they are, the more the chest muscles must work.

If the full push-up is too difficult, start with half push-ups ("kneeling push-ups"), pushing up from the knees upwards. When you can do twenty of these without having to stop, move on to full push-ups.

Sit-ups develop the stomach muscles. In the beginning it is easier to do sit-ups with your feet hooked under something (or with someone holding your ankles down) to give you more leverage. Remember to keep your knees bent at all times.

PUSH-UPS
With your hands under your shoulders, raise your shoulders gently from the ground. This exercises the chest muscles.

Keep your ankles, knees, hips and back in a straight line. Lower yourself gently. Repeat as many times as you can without straining yourself.

Hands behind neck, knees bent. Raise shoulders and curl the trunk forward from the neck as much as possible to strengthen the stomach muscles.

Keeping your feet high, on a bench, against a wall or under parallel bars means that you are putting more weight on your body when you do trunk curls.

PULL-UPS
Pull-ups are really tough exercises to strengthen your forearms and biceps. Take it very gently in the beginning and do not over-strain. Don't cheat by jumping off the ground, but pull yourself slowly and gently up as far as you can.

When your arms are strong enough, you can chin the bar. And when you are in top trim, you can keep your hands further apart, thus making your chest muscles work harder, too.

WRIST CURLS
With your forearms supported by a bench, hold the barbell with an undergrasp (closed wrists). Flex the wrists upwards and then towards your body.

Then lower the barbell as much as possible, feeling how your wrist flexors work. Keep the forearms still and fully supported on the bench.

The reverse wrist curl is the opposite movement to the above and exercises the wrist extensors.

Make sure that you flex your wrists fully, reaching full extension at the end of each arc of movement.

ARM CURLS WITH BARBELLS
Lifting light barbells from hips to shoulders with an undergrasp to strengthen your underarm muscles (arm flexors) as well as your overarm muscles (biceps). Stand with feet slightly apart and knees flexed. Keep your elbows close to your side throughout the movement.

If you want to involve the shoulder muscles more, keep the barbell away from your body before bending your elbows.

This exercise unit works the muscles of the back and the upper arms (biceps) when the parallel-grip bar is pulled from above the head to behind the shoulders.

Pull the parallel-grip bar down in front of your chest to simulate climbing more and to exercise the muscles you would use to pull yourself up onto a ledge in a mantling movement (see pages 92–93).

Dips in a dipping station on a gym unit strengthen the arms for all kinds of climbing jobs.

Another exercise unit that exercises the pulling muscles of the arm and back. Lift the weight towards your chest and let it slowly go back to its first position.

Training

Endurance training

If you want to train a muscle's endurance and flexibility, it is better to train at 50% of the max weight, but to do five sets of forty reps. Slow, long and light work increases your endurance.

Strengthen your fingers and hands

Fingers and hands are where the beginner feels the weakest and also where overworking without being trained can lead to strains and long-lasting inflammations of joints. Train your fingers and hands for endurance and flexibility. Find a rubber ball and squeeze it at about 50% of your strength capacity and keep it squeezed for as long as you can. This is good for fingers, hand and forearm.

Another method of increasing your fingers' endurance is to find a way of loading them. For instance, you can buy finger bands that attach to each individual finger and that can be weighted with different weights. A method that has the same effect but costs nothing and actually simulates climbing is to use your body as a weight and hang by your fingers from the top of a door or suchlike. Don't try to use your whole body weight to begin with (you can't anyway). That would exert too much strain on your fingers and forearms. Instead, support most of your body on your feet and hang only as much of your weight on your fingers as feels safe. Keep it up until you feel that you are close to your limit. Then take a break and do it again. Regular training like this will soon lead to increased endurance, and when you feel up to it you can increase the amount of body weight by transferring more weight from your feet to your hands.

Endurance training for calf and foot muscles

Strengthen your calf and foot muscles by rising up on your toes and then lowering. Do it slowly and as many times as you can. Yet another exercise that simulates climbing is the static toe stand. Find a suitable ledge, such as a step of the stairs, and stand on it facing the stairs with your toes pointing in the same direction. Keep your heels lower than your toes and stay in this position for as long as you can. Then stand for as long as you can on the inside edges of your big toes (heels apart and toes pointing in opposite directions), using your hands to hold balance.

Flexibility and stretching

Too much strength training can lead to short, stiff muscle fibres, if the training is not interspersed with stretching. Regular stretching will increase your flexibility.

The contract-relax-contract method is excellent flexibility

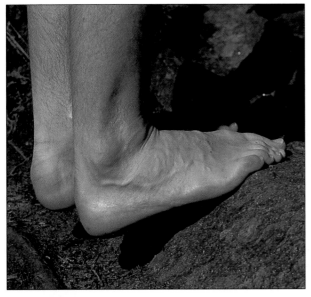

STATIC EXERCISING
Standing still with toes on ledge. Heels slightly lower than toes.

Raise yourself up on your toes and hold it as long as you can. Use hands for balance only, not support.

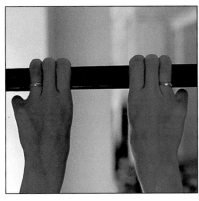

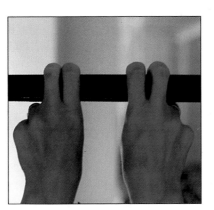

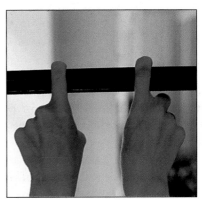

FINGER STRENGTHENERS
Tendinitis caused by cling grips on minimal holds is one of the most common climbing injuries. Developing finger strength helps avoid this. Do your finger workouts with care and use some kind of foot support to take your full weight. As your finger strength increases over the months, allow more and more of your body weight to hang on your fingers.

(Above left) Dead hangs with three fingers of each hand. Not your full body weight to begin with.

Dead hangs with two fingers of each hand.

And with one finger of each hand. Use a lot of foot support!

training. Say that you want to increase the flexibility of your deltoids (the shoulder muscles that too often get stiff from sitting in front of a computer and from strength training with weights). You do not need any expensive equipment, a short piece of old climbing rope or accessory cord will do. Take the rope and hold one end in each hand as if you were going to dry your back. First, without pulling at the rope, contract all your shoulder muscles for ten seconds, then relax them for about four seconds, and finally pull your hands away from each other hard and "dry your back" for ten seconds. Do this ten times with the right arm uppermost and ten times with the left arm uppermost.

Do the same thing, finding suitable ways of stretching, with all the other muscle groups in your body, especially the various muscles around your thighs and hips.

Every training session should be ended with a good ten-minute stretching session like this.

Mental training

One often reads of élite sportsmen who reach new heights of excellence by mental training. In some sports, such as athletics, golf and tennis, mental training is a given part of training. So far, there is no specially prepared mental-training material for climbers, but there are several general books on aspects of mental training that the climber can certainly find useful.

Just because you are physically fit does not mean that you automatically have all that is needed to become a good climber. As many experienced climbers willingly emphasize, it is often your mental attitude (fear of falling, lack of self-confidence, inability to "see" yourself succeeding) rather than your lack of physical fitness that stops your progress on a particularly tough route. You can always train in the gym to increase your arm strength with a view to solving a particular crux or by simulating the problem at a boulder or indoor wall, but when you get out on the climb again it might still be beyond you, due to the fact that you have not convinced yourself that you are actually going to make it.

All climbers experience fear at some stage or other. Mental training can teach you to handle this fear positively and thus develop a more confident approach to climbing and to life in general.

Grading climbs

A route's grade and name are first decided by whoever climbs it first. Name and grade are then entered in the guide book for the area (usually kept up-to-date by the local climbing organization). The idea is that beginners and visiting climbers can use the grading when picking suitable routes to climb.

To begin with, a grading is purely subjective – the personal opinion of the team which first climbed it. If the team is highly experienced and skilled then they may grade it too low. When a number of other climbers have tried the route, the consensus of opinion may lead to the grading being changed. Oddly enough, this happens rarely, as climbers tend to agree on the difficulty of any particular route, which is strange, given the wide range of skill and experience among climbers.

The chart attempts to compare some grading systems. It is impossible to make a completely accurate comparison, of course.

British system (in words)	British system (in figures)	American YDS-system	American NCCS–system	UIAA	Australia
Easy (E)		1, 2	F1	I	1, 2
Moderate (Mod)	1a 1b 1c	3 4 5.0	F2 F3	II III– III	3 4 5
Difficult (Diff)	2a 2b	5.1 5.2	F4	III+ IV–	6 7
Very difficult (V diff)	2c 3a	5.3 5.4	F5	IV IV+	8 9, 10
Severe (S)	3b 4a	5.5 5.6	F6	V– V	11, 12 13, 14
Very severe (VS)	4b 4c	5.7 5.8	F7 F8	V+ VI–	15, 16 17
Hard Very severe (HVS)	5a 5b	5.9	F9	VI	18, 19 20
Mild Extremely severe (E1)	5c	5.10a 5.10b	F10	VII	21 22
Mild Extremely severe (E2)		5.10c 5.10d	F11		23 24
Extremely severe (E3)	6a 6b	5.11a 5.11b	F12	VIII	25 26
Extremely severe (E4)	6c	5.11c 5.11d	F13		27 28
Hard Extremely Severe (E5)	7a	5.12a 5.12b			29 30
Hard Extremely severe (E6)	7b	5.12c 5.12d		IX	31 32
Hard Extremely Severe (E7)	7c	5.13			33

Bibliography

Barry, John & Shepherd, Nigel. *Rock Climbing*. Salamander, London & New York, 1988

Cinnamon, Jerry. *Climbing Rock and Ice*. Ragged Mountain Press, Camden, Maine, USA. 1994.

John Forrest Gregory. *Rock Sport*. Stackpole Books, Mechanicsburg, PA, USA, 1989.

Fyffe, Allen & Peter, Iain. *The Handbook of Climbing*. Pelham Books, London, 1990.

Hurn, Martin & Ingle, Pat. *Climbing Fit*. Crowood Press, Marlborough, Wilts., England, 1988.

Long, John. *How to Rock Climb*. Chockstone Press, Boulder, Colorado, USA. 1989.
– *Face Climbing*. Chockstone Press, Boulder, Colorado, USA. 1991.
– *Climbing Anchors*. Chockstone Press, Boulder, Colorado, USA. 1993.
– *Face and Sport Climbing*. Chockstone Press, Boulder, Colorado, USA. 1994.

Shepherd, Nigel. *A Manual of Modern Rope Techniques*. Constable, London, 1990.

Index

Numbers in *italics* refer to illustrations